Performance testing
Complete Self-Assessment Guide

C000003902

The guidance in this Self-Assessment is based on Performance testing best practices and standards in business process architecture, design and quality management. The guidance is also based on the professional judgment of the individual collaborators listed in the Acknowledgments.

Notice of rights

Trademarks

Table of Contents

About The Art of Service

The Art of Service, Business Process Architects since 2000, is dedicated to helping stakeholders achieve excellence.

Defining, designing, creating, and implementing a process to solve a stakeholders challenge or meet an objective is the most valuable role... In EVERY group, company, organization and department.

Unless you're talking a one-time, single-use project, there should be a process. Whether that process is managed and implemented by humans, AI, or a combination of the two, it needs to be designed by someone with a complex enough perspective to ask the right questions.

Someone capable of asking the right questions and step back and say, 'What are we really trying to accomplish here? And is there a different way to look at it?'

With The Art of Service's Standard Requirements Self-Assessments, we empower people who can do just that — whether their title is marketer, entrepreneur, manager, salesperson, consultant, Business Process Manager, executive assistant, IT Manager, CIO etc... —they are the people who rule the future. They are people who watch the process as it happens, and ask the right questions to make the process work better.

Contact us when you need any support with this Self-Assessment and any help with templates, blue-prints and examples of standard documents you might need:

http://theartofservice.com
service@theartofservice.com

Acknowledgments

This checklist was developed under the auspices of The Art of Service, chaired by Gerardus Blokdyk.

Representatives from several client companies participated in the preparation of this Self-Assessment.

In addition, we are thankful for the design and printing services provided.

Included Resources - how to access

Included with your purchase of the book is the Performance testing Self-Assessment Spreadsheet Dashboard which contains all questions and Self-Assessment areas and auto-generates insights, graphs, and project RACI planning - all with examples to get you started right away.

How? Simply send an email to
access@theartofservice.com
with this books' title in the subject to get the Performance testing Self Assessment Tool right away.

You will receive the following contents with New and Updated specific criteria:

- The latest quick edition of the book in PDF

- The latest complete edition of the book in PDF, which criteria correspond to the criteria in...

- The Self-Assessment Excel Dashboard, and...

- Example pre-filled Self-Assessment Excel Dashboard to get familiar with results generation

- In-depth specific Checklists covering the topic

- Project management checklists and templates to assist with implementation

INCLUDES LIFETIME SELF ASSESSMENT UPDATES

Every self assessment comes with Lifetime Updates and Lifetime Free Updated Books. Lifetime Updates is an industry-first feature which allows you to receive verified self assessment updates, ensuring you always have the most accurate information at your fingertips.

Get it now- you will be glad you did - do it now, before you forget.

Send an email to **access@theartofservice.com** with this books' title in the subject to get the Performance testing Self Assessment Tool right away.

Your feedback is invaluable to us

If you recently bought this book, we would love to hear from you! You can do this by writing a review on amazon (or the online store where you purchased this book) about your last purchase! As part of our continual service improvement process, we love to hear real client experiences and feedback.

How does it work?

To post a review on Amazon, just log in to your account and click on the Create Your Own Review button (under Customer Reviews) of the relevant product page. You can find examples of product reviews in Amazon. If you purchased from another online store, simply follow their procedures.

What happens when I submit my review?

Once you have submitted your review, send us an email at review@theartofservice.com with the link to your review so we can properly thank you for your feedback.

Purpose of this Self-Assessment

This Self-Assessment has been developed to improve understanding of the requirements and elements of Performance testing, based on best practices and standards in business process architecture, design and quality management.

It is designed to allow for a rapid Self-Assessment to determine how closely existing management practices and procedures correspond to the elements of the Self-Assessment.

The criteria of requirements and elements of Performance testing have been rephrased in the format of a Self-Assessment questionnaire, with a seven-criterion scoring system, as explained in this document.

In this format, even with limited background knowledge of

Performance testing, a manager can quickly review existing operations to determine how they measure up to the standards. This in turn can serve as the starting point of a 'gap analysis' to identify management tools or system elements that might usefully be implemented in the organization to help improve overall performance.

How to use the Self-Assessment

On the following pages are a series of questions to identify to what extent your Performance testing initiative is complete in comparison to the requirements set in standards.

To facilitate answering the questions, there is a space in front of each question to enter a score on a scale of '1' to '5'.

1 Strongly Disagree

2 Disagree

3 Neutral

4 Agree

5 Strongly Agree

Read the question and rate it with the following in front of mind:

'In my belief, the answer to this question is clearly defined'.

There are two ways in which you can choose to interpret this statement;
1. how aware are you that the answer to the question is clearly defined
2. for more in-depth analysis you can choose to gather

evidence and confirm the answer to the question. This obviously will take more time, most Self-Assessment users opt for the first way to interpret the question and dig deeper later on based on the outcome of the overall Self-Assessment.

A score of '1' would mean that the answer is not clear at all, where a '5' would mean the answer is crystal clear and defined. Leave emtpy when the question is not applicable or you don't want to answer it, you can skip it without affecting your score. Write your score in the space provided.

After you have responded to all the appropriate statements in each section, compute your average score for that section, using the formula provided, and round to the nearest tenth. Then transfer to the corresponding spoke in the Performance testing Scorecard on the second next page of the Self-Assessment.

Your completed Performance testing Scorecard will give you a clear presentation of which Performance testing areas need attention.

Performance testing Scorecard Example

Example of how the finalized Scorecard can look like:

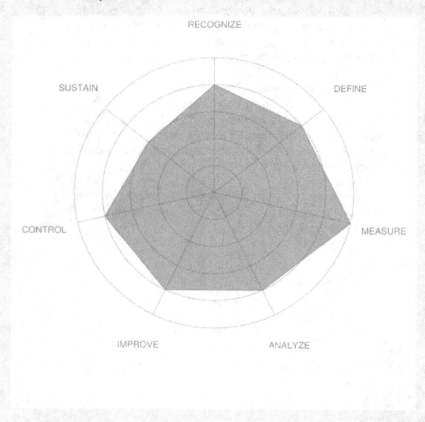

Performance testing
Scorecard

Your Scores:

BEGINNING OF THE SELF-ASSESSMENT:

CRITERION #1: RECOGNIZE

INTENT: Be aware of the need for change. Recognize that there is an unfavorable variation, problem or symptom.

In my belief, the answer to this question is clearly defined:

5 Strongly Agree

4 Agree

3 Neutral

2 Disagree

1 Strongly Disagree

1. What do you need to start doing?
<--- Score

2. Can management personnel recognize the monetary benefit of Performance testing?
<--- Score

3. Who defines the rules in relation to any given issue?
<--- Score

4. What vendors make products that address the Performance testing needs?
<--- Score

5. What problems are you facing and how do you consider Performance testing will circumvent those obstacles?
<--- Score

6. Looking at each person individually – does every one have the qualities which are needed to work in this group?
<--- Score

7. What problems do you need to solve with performance testing?
<--- Score

8. Are there any revenue recognition issues?
<--- Score

9. Have you identified your Performance testing key performance indicators?
<--- Score

10. To what extent does each concerned units management team recognize Performance testing as an effective investment?
<--- Score

11. Are there Performance testing problems defined?
<--- Score

12. Who else hopes to benefit from it?
<--- Score

13. What extra resources will you need?
<--- Score

14. What would happen if Performance testing weren't done?
<--- Score

15. What is the smallest subset of the problem you can usefully solve?
<--- Score

16. Does Performance testing create potential expectations in other areas that need to be recognized and considered?
<--- Score

17. What training and capacity building actions are needed to implement proposed reforms?
<--- Score

18. To what extent would your organization benefit from being recognized as a award recipient?
<--- Score

19. Are there recognized Performance testing problems?
<--- Score

20. What does Performance testing success mean to the stakeholders?
<--- Score

21. When a Performance testing manager recognizes a problem, what options are available?
<--- Score

22. Are your goals realistic? Do you need to redefine your problem? Perhaps the problem has changed or maybe you have reached your goal and need to set a new one?
<--- Score

23. How do you assess your Performance testing workforce capability and capacity needs, including skills, competencies, and staffing levels?
<--- Score

24. For your Performance testing project, identify and describe the business environment, is there more than one layer to the business environment?
<--- Score

25. Who needs to know about Performance testing?
<--- Score

26. Will a response program recognize when a crisis occurs and provide some level of response?
<--- Score

27. Does your organization need more Performance testing education?
<--- Score

28. What needs to be done?
<--- Score

29. Who needs what information?
<--- Score

30. As a sponsor, customer or management, how important is it to meet goals, objectives?

<--- Score

31. Will it solve real problems?
<--- Score

32. How do you identify the kinds of information that you will need?
<--- Score

33. How does it fit into your organizational needs and tasks?
<--- Score

34. How much are sponsors, customers, partners, stakeholders involved in Performance testing? In other words, what are the risks, if Performance testing does not deliver successfully?
<--- Score

35. Do you need to avoid or amend any Performance testing activities?
<--- Score

36. Are problem definition and motivation clearly presented?
<--- Score

37. Which information does the Performance testing business case need to include?
<--- Score

38. What information do users need?
<--- Score

39. How do you take a forward-looking perspective in identifying Performance testing research related to

market response and models?
<--- Score

40. What is the problem or issue?
<--- Score

41. Will new equipment/products be required to facilitate Performance testing delivery, for example is new software needed?
<--- Score

42. What are your needs in relation to Performance testing skills, labor, equipment, and markets?
<--- Score

43. Is the need for organizational change recognized?
<--- Score

44. Do you have/need 24-hour access to key personnel?
<--- Score

45. What are the minority interests and what amount of minority interests can be recognized?
<--- Score

46. Are controls defined to recognize and contain problems?
<--- Score

47. What else needs to be measured?
<--- Score

48. What should be considered when identifying available resources, constraints, and deadlines?
<--- Score

49. Are you dealing with any of the same issues today as yesterday? What can you do about this?
<--- Score

50. Think about the people you identified for your Performance testing project and the project responsibilities you would assign to them, what kind of training do you think they would need to perform these responsibilities effectively?
<--- Score

51. Is it clear when you think of the day ahead of you what activities and tasks you need to complete?
<--- Score

52. What tools and technologies are needed for a custom Performance testing project?
<--- Score

53. What situation(s) led to this Performance testing Self Assessment?
<--- Score

54. What are the stakeholder objectives to be achieved with Performance testing?
<--- Score

55. How can auditing be a preventative security measure?
<--- Score

56. What are the expected benefits of Performance testing to the stakeholder?
<--- Score

57. Do you know what you need to know about Performance testing?
<--- Score

58. Are employees recognized or rewarded for performance that demonstrates the highest levels of integrity?
<--- Score

59. Will Performance testing deliverables need to be tested and, if so, by whom?
<--- Score

60. How are the Performance testing's objectives aligned to the group's overall stakeholder strategy?
<--- Score

61. What are the timeframes required to resolve each of the issues/problems?
<--- Score

62. What activities does the governance board need to consider?
<--- Score

63. How are you going to measure success?
<--- Score

64. What is the Performance testing problem definition? What do you need to resolve?
<--- Score

65. What prevents you from making the changes you know will make you a more effective Performance testing leader?
<--- Score

66. Are there any specific expectations or concerns about the Performance testing team, Performance testing itself?
<--- Score

67. Who are your key stakeholders who need to sign off?
<--- Score

68. Do you need different information or graphics?
<--- Score

69. Consider your own Performance testing project, what types of organizational problems do you think might be causing or affecting your problem, based on the work done so far?
<--- Score

Add up total points for this section:
_____ = Total points for this section

Divided by: _____ (number of statements answered) = _____ Average score for this section

Transfer your score to the Performance testing Index at the beginning of the Self-Assessment.

CRITERION #2: DEFINE:

INTENT: Formulate the stakeholder problem. Define the problem, needs and objectives.

In my belief, the answer to this question is clearly defined:

5 Strongly Agree

4 Agree

3 Neutral

2 Disagree

1 Strongly Disagree

1. Who is gathering information?
<--- Score

2. Has your scope been defined?
<--- Score

3. Is it clearly defined in and to your organization what you do?
<--- Score

4. What sort of initial information to gather?
<--- Score

5. What are the tasks and definitions?
<--- Score

6. What constraints exist that might impact the team?
<--- Score

7. What are the compelling stakeholder reasons for embarking on Performance testing?
<--- Score

8. Have all basic functions of Performance testing been defined?
<--- Score

9. Is the team sponsored by a champion or stakeholder leader?
<--- Score

10. What is the scope?
<--- Score

11. Are team charters developed?
<--- Score

12. Have all of the relationships been defined properly?
<--- Score

13. What are the dynamics of the communication plan?
<--- Score

14. Does the scope remain the same?
<--- Score

15. What key stakeholder process output measure(s) does Performance testing leverage and how?
<--- Score

16. What is the definition of success?
<--- Score

17. What is in scope?
<--- Score

18. What defines best in class?
<--- Score

19. How do you gather requirements?
<--- Score

20. Is there a clear Performance testing case definition?
<--- Score

21. Who defines (or who defined) the rules and roles?
<--- Score

22. What is in the scope and what is not in scope?
<--- Score

23. When are meeting minutes sent out? Who is on the distribution list?
<--- Score

24. Is scope creep really all bad news?
<--- Score

25. What are the rough order estimates on cost savings/opportunities that Performance testing brings?
<--- Score

26. Who is gathering Performance testing information?
<--- Score

27. Have specific policy objectives been defined?
<--- Score

28. Has everyone on the team, including the team leaders, been properly trained?
<--- Score

29. How did the Performance testing manager receive input to the development of a Performance testing improvement plan and the estimated completion dates/times of each activity?
<--- Score

30. Will a Performance testing production readiness review be required?
<--- Score

31. What is out of scope?
<--- Score

32. Do the problem and goal statements meet the SMART criteria (specific, measurable, attainable, relevant, and time-bound)?
<--- Score

33. Are resources adequate for the scope?
<--- Score

34. What intelligence can you gather?
<--- Score

35. Is there a Performance testing management charter, including stakeholder case, problem and goal statements, scope, milestones, roles and responsibilities, communication plan?
<--- Score

36. How do you hand over Performance testing context?
<--- Score

37. Who are the Performance testing improvement team members, including Management Leads and Coaches?
<--- Score

38. How does the Performance testing manager ensure against scope creep?
<--- Score

39. What sources do you use to gather information for a Performance testing study?
<--- Score

40. What are the boundaries of the scope? What is in bounds and what is not? What is the start point? What is the stop point?
<--- Score

41. Are improvement team members fully trained on Performance testing?
<--- Score

42. Are there different segments of customers?
<--- Score

43. Is the Performance testing scope complete and appropriately sized?
<--- Score

44. Are different versions of process maps needed to account for the different types of inputs?
<--- Score

45. Is Performance testing required?
<--- Score

46. Is there any additional Performance testing definition of success?
<--- Score

47. How will the Performance testing team and the group measure complete success of Performance testing?
<--- Score

48. Is performance Testing in Scope?
<--- Score

49. Will team members regularly document their Performance testing work?
<--- Score

50. How do you catch Performance testing definition inconsistencies?
<--- Score

51. Has a Performance testing requirement not been met?

<--- Score

52. If substitutes have been appointed, have they been briefed on the Performance testing goals and received regular communications as to the progress to date?
<--- Score

53. Where can you gather more information?
<--- Score

54. Is data collected and displayed to better understand customer(s) critical needs and requirements.
<--- Score

55. What scope do you want your strategy to cover?
<--- Score

56. What scope to assess?
<--- Score

57. What are the Roles and Responsibilities for each team member and its leadership? Where is this documented?
<--- Score

58. What information should you gather?
<--- Score

59. Are there any constraints known that bear on the ability to perform Performance testing work? How is the team addressing them?
<--- Score

60. When is the estimated completion date?

<--- Score

61. Is performance testing of reporting component in scope?
<--- Score

62. How will variation in the actual durations of each activity be dealt with to ensure that the expected Performance testing results are met?
<--- Score

63. Has a high-level 'as is' process map been completed, verified and validated?
<--- Score

64. Are task requirements clearly defined?
<--- Score

65. Are approval levels defined for contracts and supplements to contracts?
<--- Score

66. How do you keep key subject matter experts in the loop?
<--- Score

67. Are customer(s) identified and segmented according to their different needs and requirements?
<--- Score

68. What is the definition of Performance testing excellence?
<--- Score

69. Scope of sensitive information?
<--- Score

70. What are the core elements of the Performance testing business case?
<--- Score

71. How do you manage scope?
<--- Score

72. Do you all define Performance testing in the same way?
<--- Score

73. Is the scope of Performance testing defined?
<--- Score

74. What are the Performance testing use cases?
<--- Score

75. What Performance testing services do you require?
<--- Score

76. How would you define Performance testing leadership?
<--- Score

77. Is full participation by members in regularly held team meetings guaranteed?
<--- Score

78. Is performance testing required for the interfaces?
<--- Score

79. What system do you use for gathering Performance testing information?
<--- Score

80. What are the Performance testing tasks and definitions?
<--- Score

81. How do you manage changes in Performance testing requirements?
<--- Score

82. Has the improvement team collected the 'voice of the customer' (obtained feedback – qualitative and quantitative)?
<--- Score

83. Is there a completed SIPOC representation, describing the Suppliers, Inputs, Process, Outputs, and Customers?
<--- Score

84. Why are you doing Performance testing and what is the scope?
<--- Score

85. Are roles and responsibilities formally defined?
<--- Score

86. How was the 'as is' process map developed, reviewed, verified and validated?
<--- Score

87. Are accountability and ownership for Performance testing clearly defined?
<--- Score

88. Will team members perform Performance testing work when assigned and in a timely fashion?

<--- Score

89. Have the customer needs been translated into specific, measurable requirements? How?
<--- Score

90. Testing - is performance testing in scope?
<--- Score

91. Are audit criteria, scope, frequency and methods defined?
<--- Score

92. What specifically is the problem? Where does it occur? When does it occur? What is its extent?
<--- Score

93. Is the Performance testing scope manageable?
<--- Score

94. What baselines are required to be defined and managed?
<--- Score

95. Is special Performance testing user knowledge required?
<--- Score

96. Is the current 'as is' process being followed? If not, what are the discrepancies?
<--- Score

97. What are the record-keeping requirements of Performance testing activities?
<--- Score

98. Is the improvement team aware of the different versions of a process: what they think it is vs. what it actually is vs. what it should be vs. what it could be?
<--- Score

99. Has/have the customer(s) been identified?
<--- Score

100. How would you define the culture at your organization, how susceptible is it to Performance testing changes?
<--- Score

101. What is the worst case scenario?
<--- Score

102. Has a project plan, Gantt chart, or similar been developed/completed?
<--- Score

103. What customer feedback methods were used to solicit their input?
<--- Score

104. Has the Performance testing work been fairly and/or equitably divided and delegated among team members who are qualified and capable to perform the work? Has everyone contributed?
<--- Score

105. How is the team tracking and documenting its work?
<--- Score

106. Has anyone else (internal or external to the group) attempted to solve this problem or a similar

one before? If so, what knowledge can be leveraged from these previous efforts?
<--- Score

107. What critical content must be communicated – who, what, when, where, and how?
<--- Score

108. The political context: who holds power?
<--- Score

109. Does the team have regular meetings?
<--- Score

110. How do you gather Performance testing requirements?
<--- Score

111. How can the value of Performance testing be defined?
<--- Score

112. What is the context?
<--- Score

113. How have you defined all Performance testing requirements first?
<--- Score

114. Is there a completed, verified, and validated high-level 'as is' (not 'should be' or 'could be') stakeholder process map?
<--- Score

115. Are customers identified and high impact areas defined?

<--- Score

116. Are required metrics defined, what are they?
<--- Score

117. How are consistent Performance testing definitions important?
<--- Score

118. What information do you gather?
<--- Score

119. Has the direction changed at all during the course of Performance testing? If so, when did it change and why?
<--- Score

120. What is out-of-scope initially?
<--- Score

121. Is the team formed and are team leaders (Coaches and Management Leads) assigned?
<--- Score

122. What was the context?
<--- Score

123. How do you gather the stories?
<--- Score

124. What happens if Performance testing's scope changes?
<--- Score

125. Has a team charter been developed and communicated?

<--- Score

126. Are stakeholder processes mapped?
<--- Score

127. Is Performance testing linked to key stakeholder goals and objectives?
<--- Score

128. In what way can you redefine the criteria of choice clients have in your category in your favor?
<--- Score

129. When is/was the Performance testing start date?
<--- Score

130. Is Performance testing currently on schedule according to the plan?
<--- Score

131. Is a fully trained team formed, supported, and committed to work on the Performance testing improvements?
<--- Score

132. What is the scope of Performance testing?
<--- Score

133. What is the scope of the Performance testing effort?
<--- Score

134. Is there a critical path to deliver Performance testing results?
<--- Score

135. Is there regularly 100% attendance at the team meetings? If not, have appointed substitutes attended to preserve cross-functionality and full representation?
<--- Score

136. How and when will the baselines be defined?
<--- Score

137. What would be the goal or target for a Performance testing's improvement team?
<--- Score

138. Is the team adequately staffed with the desired cross-functionality? If not, what additional resources are available to the team?
<--- Score

139. Is the team equipped with available and reliable resources?
<--- Score

140. How do you think the partners involved in Performance testing would have defined success?
<--- Score

141. What Performance testing requirements should be gathered?
<--- Score

142. Do you have a Performance testing success story or case study ready to tell and share?
<--- Score

143. How often are the team meetings?
<--- Score

144. How do you manage unclear Performance testing requirements?
<--- Score

Add up total points for this section:
_ _ _ _ _ = Total points for this section

Divided by: _ _ _ _ _ _ (number of statements answered) = _ _ _ _ _ _
Average score for this section

Transfer your score to the Performance testing Index at the beginning of the Self-Assessment.

CRITERION #3: MEASURE:

INTENT: Gather the correct data. Measure the current performance and evolution of the situation.

In my belief, the answer to this question is clearly defined:

5 Strongly Agree

4 Agree

3 Neutral

2 Disagree

1 Strongly Disagree

1. Is key measure data collection planned and executed, process variation displayed and communicated and performance baselined?
<--- Score

2. How much does it cost?
<--- Score

3. What drives O&M cost?

<--- Score

4. How can you measure Performance testing in a systematic way?
<--- Score

5. How do your measurements capture actionable Performance testing information for use in exceeding your customers expectations and securing your customers engagement?
<--- Score

6. What are the operational costs after Performance testing deployment?
<--- Score

7. Did you tackle the cause or the symptom?
<--- Score

8. How frequently do you verify your Performance testing strategy?
<--- Score

9. Is Process Variation Displayed/Communicated?
<--- Score

10. Among the Performance testing product and service cost to be estimated, which is considered hardest to estimate?
<--- Score

11. How do you identify and analyze stakeholders and their interests?
<--- Score

12. What are the agreed upon definitions of the high

impact areas, defect(s), unit(s), and opportunities that will figure into the process capability metrics?
<--- Score

13. What are allowable costs?
<--- Score

14. What causes investor action?
<--- Score

15. How do you measure success?
<--- Score

16. Does Performance testing analysis isolate the fundamental causes of problems?
<--- Score

17. Have all non-recommended alternatives been analyzed in sufficient detail?
<--- Score

18. Why do the measurements/indicators matter?
<--- Score

19. What do you measure and why?
<--- Score

20. How can a Performance testing test verify your ideas or assumptions?
<--- Score

21. Why do you expend time and effort to implement measurement, for whom?
<--- Score

22. What are the costs of delaying Performance

testing action?
<--- Score

23. Are the measurements objective?
<--- Score

24. Are missed Performance testing opportunities costing your organization money?
<--- Score

25. Who is involved in verifying compliance?
<--- Score

26. How do you aggregate measures across priorities?
<--- Score

27. What does verifying compliance entail?
<--- Score

28. Was a life-cycle cost analysis performed?
<--- Score

29. What are the types and number of measures to use?
<--- Score

30. Are key measures identified and agreed upon?
<--- Score

31. Is data collected on key measures that were identified?
<--- Score

32. Does Performance testing analysis show the relationships among important Performance testing factors?

<--- Score

33. Are there competing Performance testing priorities?
<--- Score

34. What is your cost benefit analysis?
<--- Score

35. What do people want to verify?
<--- Score

36. What would it cost to replace your technology?
<--- Score

37. When are costs are incurred?
<--- Score

38. Do staff have the necessary skills to collect, analyze, and report data?
<--- Score

39. Does Performance testing systematically track and analyze outcomes for accountability and quality improvement?
<--- Score

40. Are process variation components displayed/communicated using suitable charts, graphs, plots?
<--- Score

41. What could cause delays in the schedule?
<--- Score

42. Does your organization systematically track and analyze outcomes related for accountability and

quality improvement?
<--- Score

43. What is the right balance of time and resources between investigation, analysis, and discussion and dissemination?
<--- Score

44. What data was collected (past, present, future/ongoing)?
<--- Score

45. Is it possible to estimate the impact of unanticipated complexity such as wrong or failed assumptions, feedback, etcetera on proposed reforms?
<--- Score

46. What kind of analytics data will be gathered?
<--- Score

47. How do you prevent mis-estimating cost?
<--- Score

48. Do the benefits outweigh the costs?
<--- Score

49. How will you measure your Performance testing effectiveness?
<--- Score

50. What are the costs and benefits?
<--- Score

51. Are you taking your company in the direction of better and revenue or cheaper and cost?

<--- Score

52. What is your decision requirements diagram?
<--- Score

53. At what cost?
<--- Score

54. What relevant entities could be measured?
<--- Score

55. How do you measure variability?
<--- Score

56. What could cause you to change course?
<--- Score

57. Do you verify that corrective actions were taken?
<--- Score

58. How large is the gap between current performance and the customer-specified (goal) performance?
<--- Score

59. How will your organization measure success?
<--- Score

60. How can you manage cost down?
<--- Score

61. Will Performance testing have an impact on current business continuity, disaster recovery processes and/or infrastructure?
<--- Score

62. What is an unallowable cost?
<--- Score

63. What happens if cost savings do not materialize?
<--- Score

64. Have changes been properly/adequately analyzed for effect?
<--- Score

65. Where is it measured?
<--- Score

66. When is Root Cause Analysis Required?
<--- Score

67. What does losing customers cost your organization?
<--- Score

68. Who should receive measurement reports?
<--- Score

69. Are high impact defects defined and identified in the stakeholder process?
<--- Score

70. What potential environmental factors impact the Performance testing effort?
<--- Score

71. What methods are feasible and acceptable to estimate the impact of reforms?
<--- Score

72. How do you quantify and qualify impacts?

<--- Score

73. Can you do Performance testing without complex (expensive) analysis?
<--- Score

74. Have you included everything in your Performance testing cost models?
<--- Score

75. The approach of traditional Performance testing works for detail complexity but is focused on a systematic approach rather than an understanding of the nature of systems themselves, what approach will permit your organization to deal with the kind of unpredictable emergent behaviors that dynamic complexity can introduce?
<--- Score

76. Have you found any 'ground fruit' or 'low-hanging fruit' for immediate remedies to the gap in performance?
<--- Score

77. What is the total cost related to deploying Performance testing, including any consulting or professional services?
<--- Score

78. How will success or failure be measured?
<--- Score

79. What measurements are possible, practicable and meaningful?
<--- Score

80. Has a cost center been established?
<--- Score

81. What are your operating costs?
<--- Score

82. How are costs allocated?
<--- Score

83. How is performance measured?
<--- Score

84. Can you measure the return on analysis?
<--- Score

85. Do you aggressively reward and promote the people who have the biggest impact on creating excellent Performance testing services/products?
<--- Score

86. Do you effectively measure and reward individual and team performance?
<--- Score

87. Are you able to realize any cost savings?
<--- Score

88. When a disaster occurs, who gets priority?
<--- Score

89. What evidence is there and what is measured?
<--- Score

90. What measurements are being captured?
<--- Score

91. Are you aware of what could cause a problem?
<--- Score

92. What has the team done to assure the stability and accuracy of the measurement process?
<--- Score

93. What are the current costs of the Performance testing process?
<--- Score

94. Are indirect costs charged to the Performance testing program?
<--- Score

95. What tests verify requirements?
<--- Score

96. Which stakeholder characteristics are analyzed?
<--- Score

97. How sensitive must the Performance testing strategy be to cost?
<--- Score

98. Does the Performance testing task fit the client's priorities?
<--- Score

99. What are the Performance testing key cost drivers?
<--- Score

100. How are measurements made?
<--- Score

101. Have you made assumptions about the shape of

the future, particularly its impact on your customers and competitors?
<--- Score

102. Do you have any cost Performance testing limitation requirements?
<--- Score

103. How do you verify the Performance testing requirements quality?
<--- Score

104. Have design-to-cost goals been established?
<--- Score

105. What disadvantage does this cause for the user?
<--- Score

106. What is the cost of rework?
<--- Score

107. How do you verify Performance testing completeness and accuracy?
<--- Score

108. What are the uncertainties surrounding estimates of impact?
<--- Score

109. Do you have a flow diagram of what happens?
<--- Score

110. What is your Performance testing quality cost segregation study?
<--- Score

111. Which costs should be taken into account?
<--- Score

112. Has a cost benefit analysis been performed?
<--- Score

113. What are the costs of reform?
<--- Score

114. Is a follow-up focused external Performance testing review required?
<--- Score

115. How is the value delivered by Performance testing being measured?
<--- Score

116. Is long term and short term variability accounted for?
<--- Score

117. How do you focus on what is right -not who is right?
<--- Score

118. How will you measure success?
<--- Score

119. How do you do risk analysis of rare, cascading, catastrophic events?
<--- Score

120. Are there any easy-to-implement alternatives to Performance testing? Sometimes other solutions are available that do not require the cost implications of a full-blown project?

<--- Score

121. How do you stay flexible and focused to recognize larger Performance testing results?
<--- Score

122. Who participated in the data collection for measurements?
<--- Score

123. What causes innovation to fail or succeed in your organization?
<--- Score

124. Are the Performance testing benefits worth its costs?
<--- Score

125. How do you verify the authenticity of the data and information used?
<--- Score

126. How will measures be used to manage and adapt?
<--- Score

127. Where can you go to verify the info?
<--- Score

128. How do you verify and develop ideas and innovations?
<--- Score

129. What does your operating model cost?
<--- Score

130. How do you verify your resources?
<--- Score

131. Is there a Performance Baseline?
<--- Score

132. How do you control the overall costs of your work processes?
<--- Score

133. Was a data collection plan established?
<--- Score

134. Have the concerns of stakeholders to help identify and define potential barriers been obtained and analyzed?
<--- Score

135. What key measures identified indicate the performance of the stakeholder process?
<--- Score

136. Which measures and indicators matter?
<--- Score

137. How do you measure lifecycle phases?
<--- Score

138. How to cause the change?
<--- Score

139. How do you measure efficient delivery of Performance testing services?
<--- Score

140. What are the key input variables? What are

the key process variables? What are the key output variables?
<--- Score

141. What are your key Performance testing indicators that you will measure, analyze and track?
<--- Score

142. Was a business case (cost/benefit) developed?
<--- Score

143. How are you verifying it?
<--- Score

144. How can you measure the performance?
<--- Score

145. Is the cost worth the Performance testing effort ?
<--- Score

146. Are actual costs in line with budgeted costs?
<--- Score

147. What is the total fixed cost?
<--- Score

148. What causes mismanagement?
<--- Score

149. What are your customers expectations and measures?
<--- Score

150. How can you reduce costs?
<--- Score

151. Is a solid data collection plan established that includes measurement systems analysis?
<--- Score

152. How do you verify performance?
<--- Score

153. What charts has the team used to display the components of variation in the process?
<--- Score

154. How do you know that any Performance testing analysis is complete and comprehensive?
<--- Score

155. Is data collection planned and executed?
<--- Score

156. How will effects be measured?
<--- Score

157. What are the estimated costs of proposed changes?
<--- Score

158. What are your primary costs, revenues, assets?
<--- Score

159. Is there an opportunity to verify requirements?
<--- Score

160. Does a Performance testing quantification method exist?
<--- Score

161. How can you reduce the costs of obtaining

inputs?

<--- Score

162. Are the units of measure consistent?

<--- Score

163. What is measured? Why?

<--- Score

164. What are your key Performance testing organizational performance measures, including key short and longer-term financial measures?

<--- Score

165. What does a Test Case verify?

<--- Score

166. How does cost-to-serve analysis help?

<--- Score

167. What would be a real cause for concern?

<--- Score

168. Have the types of risks that may impact Performance testing been identified and analyzed?

<--- Score

169. How do you verify if Performance testing is built right?

<--- Score

170. How will costs be allocated?

<--- Score

171. How is progress measured?

<--- Score

172. How frequently do you track Performance testing measures?
<--- Score

173. What harm might be caused?
<--- Score

174. What can be used to verify compliance?
<--- Score

175. What are you verifying?
<--- Score

176. Is the scope of Performance testing cost analysis cost-effective?
<--- Score

177. What causes extra work or rework?
<--- Score

178. Are there measurements based on task performance?
<--- Score

179. Are losses documented, analyzed, and remedial processes developed to prevent future losses?
<--- Score

180. When should you bother with diagrams?
<--- Score

181. What particular quality tools did the team find helpful in establishing measurements?
<--- Score

182. Are supply costs steady or fluctuating?
<--- Score

183. Is the solution cost-effective?
<--- Score

184. How do you verify and validate the Performance testing data?
<--- Score

Add up total points for this section:
_ _ _ _ _ = Total points for this section

Divided by: _ _ _ _ _ _ (number of statements answered) = _ _ _ _ _ _
Average score for this section

Transfer your score to the Performance testing Index at the beginning of the Self-Assessment.

CRITERION #4: ANALYZE:

INTENT: Analyze causes, assumptions and hypotheses.

In my belief, the answer to this question is clearly defined:

5 Strongly Agree

4 Agree

3 Neutral

2 Disagree

1 Strongly Disagree

1. Where is Performance testing data gathered?
<--- Score

2. Are all staff in core Performance testing subjects Highly Qualified?
<--- Score

3. Have the problem and goal statements been updated to reflect the additional knowledge gained from the analyze phase?

<--- Score

4. Record-keeping requirements flow from the records needed as inputs, outputs, controls and for transformation of a Performance testing process, are the records needed as inputs to the Performance testing process available?
<--- Score

5. Identify an operational issue in your organization, for example, could a particular task be done more quickly or more efficiently by Performance testing?
<--- Score

6. How do you identify specific Performance testing investment opportunities and emerging trends?
<--- Score

7. What are your best practices for minimizing Performance testing project risk, while demonstrating incremental value and quick wins throughout the Performance testing project lifecycle?
<--- Score

8. Is the performance gap determined?
<--- Score

9. Where can you get qualified talent today?
<--- Score

10. What are your key performance measures or indicators and in-process measures for the control and improvement of your Performance testing processes?
<--- Score

11. What successful thing are you doing today that may be blinding you to new growth opportunities?
<--- Score

12. Are gaps between current performance and the goal performance identified?
<--- Score

13. Are your outputs consistent?
<--- Score

14. A compounding model resolution with available relevant data can often provide insight towards a solution methodology; which Performance testing models, tools and techniques are necessary?
<--- Score

15. What resources go in to get the desired output?
<--- Score

16. Who will gather what data?
<--- Score

17. What kind of crime could a potential new hire have committed that would not only not disqualify him/her from being hired by your organization, but would actually indicate that he/she might be a particularly good fit?
<--- Score

18. What training and qualifications will you need?
<--- Score

19. Do your employees have the opportunity to do what they do best everyday?
<--- Score

20. What other jobs or tasks affect the performance of the steps in the Performance testing process?
<--- Score

21. How many input/output points does it require?
<--- Score

22. Is the gap/opportunity displayed and communicated in financial terms?
<--- Score

23. Did any additional data need to be collected?
<--- Score

24. What data is gathered?
<--- Score

25. How does the organization define, manage, and improve its Performance testing processes?
<--- Score

26. How was the detailed process map generated, verified, and validated?
<--- Score

27. How do your work systems and key work processes relate to and capitalize on your core competencies?
<--- Score

28. What tools were used to generate the list of possible causes?
<--- Score

29. How is the way you as the leader think and process

information affecting your organizational culture?
<--- Score

30. Do staff qualifications match your project?
<--- Score

31. Think about the functions involved in your Performance testing project, what processes flow from these functions?
<--- Score

32. Who is involved with workflow mapping?
<--- Score

33. How difficult is it to qualify what Performance testing ROI is?
<--- Score

34. What are evaluation criteria for the output?
<--- Score

35. Has data output been validated?
<--- Score

36. How is the data gathered?
<--- Score

37. What Performance testing metrics are outputs of the process?
<--- Score

38. What Performance testing data do you gather or use now?
<--- Score

39. What is the output?

<--- Score

40. An organizationally feasible system request is one that considers the mission, goals and objectives of the organization, key questions are: is the Performance testing solution request practical and will it solve a problem or take advantage of an opportunity to achieve company goals?
<--- Score

41. How do you measure the operational performance of your key work systems and processes, including productivity, cycle time, and other appropriate measures of process effectiveness, efficiency, and innovation?
<--- Score

42. How do mission and objectives affect the Performance testing processes of your organization?
<--- Score

43. What are the necessary qualifications?
<--- Score

44. Is data and process analysis, root cause analysis and quantifying the gap/opportunity in place?
<--- Score

45. What information qualified as important?
<--- Score

46. Are Performance testing changes recognized early enough to be approved through the regular process?
<--- Score

47. What is the cost of poor quality as supported by

the team's analysis?
<--- Score

48. What qualifications are needed?
<--- Score

49. What process should you select for improvement?
<--- Score

50. Think about some of the processes you undertake within your organization, which do you own?
<--- Score

51. What other organizational variables, such as reward systems or communication systems, affect the performance of this Performance testing process?
<--- Score

52. What will drive Performance testing change?
<--- Score

53. Have you defined which data is gathered how?
<--- Score

54. Should you invest in industry-recognized qualifications?
<--- Score

55. Was a cause-and-effect diagram used to explore the different types of causes (or sources of variation)?
<--- Score

56. What conclusions were drawn from the team's data collection and analysis? How did the team reach these conclusions?
<--- Score

57. What does the data say about the performance of the stakeholder process?
<--- Score

58. Is this a one-shot effort, or will you need to do performance testing as part of your development process for years to come?
<--- Score

59. What methods do you use to gather Performance testing data?
<--- Score

60. Where is the data coming from to measure compliance?
<--- Score

61. What are your Performance testing processes?
<--- Score

62. How often will data be collected for measures?
<--- Score

63. Were any designed experiments used to generate additional insight into the data analysis?
<--- Score

64. Do several people in different organizational units assist with the Performance testing process?
<--- Score

65. What qualifications do Performance testing leaders need?
<--- Score

66. What were the financial benefits resulting from any 'ground fruit or low-hanging fruit' (quick fixes)?
<--- Score

67. Can you add value to the current Performance testing decision-making process (largely qualitative) by incorporating uncertainty modeling (more quantitative)?
<--- Score

68. Do you, as a leader, bounce back quickly from setbacks?
<--- Score

69. What quality tools were used to get through the analyze phase?
<--- Score

70. How do you use Performance testing data and information to support organizational decision making and innovation?
<--- Score

71. What were the crucial 'moments of truth' on the process map?
<--- Score

72. How are outputs preserved and protected?
<--- Score

73. Is the required Performance testing data gathered?
<--- Score

74. Is pre-qualification of suppliers carried out?
<--- Score

75. What data do you need to collect?
<--- Score

76. Who gets your output?
<--- Score

77. Was a detailed process map created to amplify critical steps of the 'as is' stakeholder process?
<--- Score

78. Is the Performance testing process severely broken such that a re-design is necessary?
<--- Score

79. Do your contracts/agreements contain data security obligations?
<--- Score

80. What is the Value Stream Mapping?
<--- Score

81. What is your organizations system for selecting qualified vendors?
<--- Score

82. What qualifications and skills do you need?
<--- Score

83. Were there any improvement opportunities identified from the process analysis?
<--- Score

84. What are the revised rough estimates of the financial savings/opportunity for Performance testing improvements?

<--- Score

85. What did the team gain from developing a sub-process map?
<--- Score

86. How is the Performance testing Value Stream Mapping managed?
<--- Score

87. What qualifies as competition?
<--- Score

88. Were Pareto charts (or similar) used to portray the 'heavy hitters' (or key sources of variation)?
<--- Score

89. Do you have the authority to produce the output?
<--- Score

90. What is your organizations process which leads to recognition of value generation?
<--- Score

91. What are the best opportunities for value improvement?
<--- Score

92. What is the complexity of the output produced?
<--- Score

93. Is the suppliers process defined and controlled?
<--- Score

94. Has an output goal been set?
<--- Score

95. Did any value-added analysis or 'lean thinking' take place to identify some of the gaps shown on the 'as is' process map?
<--- Score

96. What controls do you have in place to protect data?
<--- Score

97. How is Performance testing data gathered?
<--- Score

98. What are your outputs?
<--- Score

99. What are your current levels and trends in key Performance testing measures or indicators of product and process performance that are important to and directly serve your customers?
<--- Score

100. What are the disruptive Performance testing technologies that enable your organization to radically change your business processes?
<--- Score

101. Who qualifies to gain access to data?
<--- Score

102. Do your leaders quickly bounce back from setbacks?
<--- Score

103. How do you implement and manage your work processes to ensure that they meet design

requirements?
<--- Score

104. Are all team members qualified for all tasks?
<--- Score

105. What qualifications are necessary?
<--- Score

106. How has the Performance testing data been gathered?
<--- Score

107. What tools were used to narrow the list of possible causes?
<--- Score

108. What are the personnel training and qualifications required?
<--- Score

109. What are your current levels and trends in key measures or indicators of Performance testing product and process performance that are important to and directly serve your customers? How do these results compare with the performance of your competitors and other organizations with similar offerings?
<--- Score

110. Is the final output clearly identified?
<--- Score

111. How do you define collaboration and team output?
<--- Score

112. What do you need to qualify?
<--- Score

113. Have any additional benefits been identified that will result from closing all or most of the gaps?
<--- Score

114. How do you promote understanding that opportunity for improvement is not criticism of the status quo, or the people who created the status quo?
<--- Score

115. What output to create?
<--- Score

Add up total points for this section:
_ _ _ _ _ = Total points for this section

Divided by: _ _ _ _ _ _ (number of statements answered) = _ _ _ _ _ _
Average score for this section

Transfer your score to the Performance testing Index at the beginning of the Self-Assessment.

CRITERION #5: IMPROVE:

INTENT: Develop a practical solution.
Innovate, establish and test the
solution and to measure the results.

In my belief, the answer to this
question is clearly defined:

5 Strongly Agree

4 Agree

3 Neutral

2 Disagree

1 Strongly Disagree

1. What attendant changes will need to be made to ensure that the solution is successful?
<--- Score

2. How does the team improve its work?
<--- Score

3. To what extent does management recognize Performance testing as a tool to increase the results?

<--- Score

4. How will the group know that the solution worked?
<--- Score

5. What are your current levels and trends in key measures or indicators of workforce and leader development?
<--- Score

6. What went well, what should change, what can improve?
<--- Score

7. Describe the design of the pilot and what tests were conducted, if any?
<--- Score

8. How risky is your organization?
<--- Score

9. Are you assessing Performance testing and risk?
<--- Score

10. How do you measure progress and evaluate training effectiveness?
<--- Score

11. Risk factors: what are the characteristics of Performance testing that make it risky?
<--- Score

12. What tools do you use once you have decided on a Performance testing strategy and more importantly how do you choose?
<--- Score

13. What needs improvement? Why?
<--- Score

14. How do you decide how much to remunerate an employee?
<--- Score

15. How do you define the solutions' scope?
<--- Score

16. Is a contingency plan established?
<--- Score

17. What error proofing will be done to address some of the discrepancies observed in the 'as is' process?
<--- Score

18. Are improved process ('should be') maps modified based on pilot data and analysis?
<--- Score

19. Do those selected for the Performance testing team have a good general understanding of what Performance testing is all about?
<--- Score

20. For estimation problems, how do you develop an estimation statement?
<--- Score

21. Who controls key decisions that will be made?
<--- Score

22. Risk Identification: What are the possible risk events your organization faces in relation to

Performance testing?
<--- Score

23. Is there a high likelihood that any recommendations will achieve their intended results?
<--- Score

24. How can you improve Performance testing?
<--- Score

25. How do you manage and improve your Performance testing work systems to deliver customer value and achieve organizational success and sustainability?
<--- Score

26. How do you link measurement and risk?
<--- Score

27. Who are the people involved in developing and implementing Performance testing?
<--- Score

28. Do you combine technical expertise with business knowledge and Performance testing Key topics include lifecycles, development approaches, requirements and how to make a business case?
<--- Score

29. How do you measure risk?
<--- Score

30. Performance testing risk decisions: whose call Is It?
<--- Score

31. Who will be responsible for making the decisions

to include or exclude requested changes once
Performance testing is underway?
<--- Score

32. What resources are required for the improvement
efforts?
<--- Score

33. What communications are necessary to support
the implementation of the solution?
<--- Score

34. What is Performance testing's impact on utilizing
the best solution(s)?
<--- Score

35. What is the team's contingency plan for potential
problems occurring in implementation?
<--- Score

36. What does the 'should be' process map/design
look like?
<--- Score

37. What were the underlying assumptions on the
cost-benefit analysis?
<--- Score

38. Is the optimal solution selected based on testing
and analysis?
<--- Score

39. For decision problems, how do you develop a
decision statement?
<--- Score

40. How do the Performance testing results compare with the performance of your competitors and other organizations with similar offerings?
<--- Score

41. Are the best solutions selected?
<--- Score

42. How do you improve Performance testing service perception, and satisfaction?
<--- Score

43. What is the magnitude of the improvements?
<--- Score

44. Does the goal represent a desired result that can be measured?
<--- Score

45. How do you improve your likelihood of success ?
<--- Score

46. Was a Performance testing charter developed?
<--- Score

47. Are there any constraints (technical, political, cultural, or otherwise) that would inhibit certain solutions?
<--- Score

48. Will the controls trigger any other risks?
<--- Score

49. What tools were used to evaluate the potential solutions?
<--- Score

50. How do you measure improved Performance testing service perception, and satisfaction?
<--- Score

51. Do you cover the five essential competencies: Communication, Collaboration,Innovation, Adaptability, and Leadership that improve an organizations ability to leverage the new Performance testing in a volatile global economy?
<--- Score

52. Is the implementation plan designed?
<--- Score

53. Is the scope clearly documented?
<--- Score

54. Who will be responsible for documenting the Performance testing requirements in detail?
<--- Score

55. Who makes the Performance testing decisions in your organization?
<--- Score

56. Are new and improved process ('should be') maps developed?
<--- Score

57. Is there a small-scale pilot for proposed improvement(s)? What conclusions were drawn from the outcomes of a pilot?
<--- Score

58. What is the Performance testing's sustainability

risk?
<--- Score

59. Explorations of the frontiers of Performance testing will help you build influence, improve Performance testing, optimize decision making, and sustain change, what is your approach?
<--- Score

60. What do you want to improve?
<--- Score

61. Is pilot data collected and analyzed?
<--- Score

62. How does the solution remove the key sources of issues discovered in the analyze phase?
<--- Score

63. How do you go about comparing Performance testing approaches/solutions?
<--- Score

64. What is the implementation plan?
<--- Score

65. Does a good decision guarantee a good outcome?
<--- Score

66. What lessons, if any, from a pilot were incorporated into the design of the full-scale solution?
<--- Score

67. How do you improve productivity?
<--- Score

68. How will the team or the process owner(s) monitor the implementation plan to see that it is working as intended?
<--- Score

69. How are policy decisions made and where?
<--- Score

70. Were any criteria developed to assist the team in testing and evaluating potential solutions?
<--- Score

71. How can you improve performance?
<--- Score

72. Are possible solutions generated and tested?
<--- Score

73. What to do with the results or outcomes of measurements?
<--- Score

74. What is the risk?
<--- Score

75. Are risk triggers captured?
<--- Score

76. Can you identify any significant risks or exposures to Performance testing third- parties (vendors, service providers, alliance partners etc) that concern you?
<--- Score

77. Are decisions made in a timely manner?
<--- Score

78. How will you know that a change is an improvement?
<--- Score

79. How will you know when its improved?
<--- Score

80. How will you know that you have improved?
<--- Score

81. How significant is the improvement in the eyes of the end user?
<--- Score

82. If you could go back in time five years, what decision would you make differently? What is your best guess as to what decision you're making today you might regret five years from now?
<--- Score

83. What tools were used to tap into the creativity and encourage 'outside the box' thinking?
<--- Score

84. What can you do to improve?
<--- Score

85. How did the team generate the list of possible solutions?
<--- Score

86. When you map the key players in your own work and the types/domains of relationships with them, which relationships do you find easy and which challenging, and why?
<--- Score

87. What actually has to improve and by how much?
<--- Score

88. What should a proof of concept or pilot accomplish?
<--- Score

89. In the past few months, what is the smallest change you have made that has had the biggest positive result? What was it about that small change that produced the large return?
<--- Score

90. How will you measure the results?
<--- Score

91. Which of the recognised risks out of all risks can be most likely transferred?
<--- Score

92. Why improve in the first place?
<--- Score

93. What tools were most useful during the improve phase?
<--- Score

94. At what point will vulnerability assessments be performed once Performance testing is put into production (e.g., ongoing Risk Management after implementation)?
<--- Score

95. Who do you report Performance testing results to?
<--- Score

96. Can the solution be designed and implemented within an acceptable time period?
<--- Score

97. Risk events: what are the things that could go wrong?
<--- Score

98. Is a solution implementation plan established, including schedule/work breakdown structure, resources, risk management plan, cost/budget, and control plan?
<--- Score

99. Was a pilot designed for the proposed solution(s)?
<--- Score

100. Is there a cost/benefit analysis of optimal solution(s)?
<--- Score

101. Have you identified breakpoints and/or risk tolerances that will trigger broad consideration of a potential need for intervention or modification of strategy?
<--- Score

102. How can skill-level changes improve Performance testing?
<--- Score

103. What practices helps your organization to develop its capacity to recognize patterns?
<--- Score

104. Who will be using the results of the measurement activities?
<--- Score

105. What improvements have been achieved?
<--- Score

106. Is the measure of success for Performance testing understandable to a variety of people?
<--- Score

107. Is the solution technically practical?
<--- Score

108. What are the implications of the one critical Performance testing decision 10 minutes, 10 months, and 10 years from now?
<--- Score

109. How do you keep improving Performance testing?
<--- Score

110. Who controls the risk?
<--- Score

111. Is supporting Performance testing documentation required?
<--- Score

Add up total points for this section:
_ _ _ _ _ = Total points for this section

Divided by: _ _ _ _ _ _ (number of
statements answered) = _ _ _ _ _ _
Average score for this section

Transfer your score to the Performance
testing Index at the beginning of the
Self-Assessment.

CRITERION #6: CONTROL:

INTENT: Implement the practical solution. Maintain the performance and correct possible complications.

In my belief, the answer to this question is clearly defined:

5 Strongly Agree

4 Agree

3 Neutral

2 Disagree

1 Strongly Disagree

1. Is there a transfer of ownership and knowledge to process owner and process team tasked with the responsibilities.
<--- Score

2. Are the planned controls in place?
<--- Score

3. What quality tools were useful in the control phase?

<--- Score

4. What adjustments to the strategies are needed?
<--- Score

5. Is there documentation that will support the successful operation of the improvement?
<--- Score

6. How can you best use all of your knowledge repositories to enhance learning and sharing?
<--- Score

7. Is knowledge gained on process shared and institutionalized?
<--- Score

8. Are new process steps, standards, and documentation ingrained into normal operations?
<--- Score

9. Is new knowledge gained imbedded in the response plan?
<--- Score

10. Is there a recommended audit plan for routine surveillance inspections of Performance testing's gains?
<--- Score

11. Are suggested corrective/restorative actions indicated on the response plan for known causes to problems that might surface?
<--- Score

12. What do your reports reflect?

<--- Score

13. What is the recommended frequency of auditing?
<--- Score

14. Who controls critical resources?
<--- Score

15. How do you establish and deploy modified action plans if circumstances require a shift in plans and rapid execution of new plans?
<--- Score

16. Is there a standardized process?
<--- Score

17. Does the response plan contain a definite closed loop continual improvement scheme (e.g., plan-do-check-act)?
<--- Score

18. How do you encourage people to take control and responsibility?
<--- Score

19. What can you control?
<--- Score

20. What are your results for key measures or indicators of the accomplishment of your Performance testing strategy and action plans, including building and strengthening core competencies?
<--- Score

21. Who is the Performance testing process owner?

<--- Score

22. How is Performance testing project cost planned, managed, monitored?
<--- Score

23. Has the improved process and its steps been standardized?
<--- Score

24. Are there documented procedures?
<--- Score

25. Are pertinent alerts monitored, analyzed and distributed to appropriate personnel?
<--- Score

26. Is there a control plan in place for sustaining improvements (short and long-term)?
<--- Score

27. What do you stand for--and what are you against?
<--- Score

28. Are you measuring, monitoring and predicting Performance testing activities to optimize operations and profitability, and enhancing outcomes?
<--- Score

29. How do controls support value?
<--- Score

30. In the case of a Performance testing project, the criteria for the audit derive from implementation objectives, an audit of a Performance testing project involves assessing whether the recommendations

outlined for implementation have been met, can you track that any Performance testing project is implemented as planned, and is it working?
<--- Score

31. Can you adapt and adjust to changing Performance testing situations?
<--- Score

32. Do the Performance testing decisions you make today help people and the planet tomorrow?
<--- Score

33. What is your theory of human motivation, and how does your compensation plan fit with that view?
<--- Score

34. Is a response plan in place for when the input, process, or output measures indicate an 'out-of-control' condition?
<--- Score

35. Who is going to spread your message?
<--- Score

36. What other areas of the group might benefit from the Performance testing team's improvements, knowledge, and learning?
<--- Score

37. What do you measure to verify effectiveness gains?
<--- Score

38. Is the Performance testing test/monitoring cost justified?

<--- Score

39. How will the process owner and team be able to hold the gains?
<--- Score

40. Does the test plan indicate how performance testing will be performed?
<--- Score

41. Does a troubleshooting guide exist or is it needed?
<--- Score

42. What are you attempting to measure/monitor?
<--- Score

43. Does the Performance testing performance meet the customer's requirements?
<--- Score

44. Is there a documented and implemented monitoring plan?
<--- Score

45. Will existing staff require re-training, for example, to learn new business processes?
<--- Score

46. Are the planned controls working?
<--- Score

47. Does job training on the documented procedures need to be part of the process team's education and training?
<--- Score

48. Do you monitor the Performance testing decisions made and fine tune them as they evolve?
<--- Score

49. What are the key elements of your Performance testing performance improvement system, including your evaluation, organizational learning, and innovation processes?
<--- Score

50. Against what alternative is success being measured?
<--- Score

51. What should the next improvement project be that is related to Performance testing?
<--- Score

52. How will new or emerging customer needs/ requirements be checked/communicated to orient the process toward meeting the new specifications and continually reducing variation?
<--- Score

53. Is a response plan established and deployed?
<--- Score

54. You may have created your quality measures at a time when you lacked resources, technology wasn't up to the required standard, or low service levels were the industry norm. Have those circumstances changed?
<--- Score

55. How do senior leaders actions reflect a commitment to the organizations Performance

testing values?
<--- Score

56. Has the Performance testing value of standards been quantified?
<--- Score

57. Is reporting being used or needed?
<--- Score

58. Are controls in place and consistently applied?
<--- Score

59. How will you measure your QA plan's effectiveness?
<--- Score

60. Are operating procedures consistent?
<--- Score

61. Act/Adjust: What Do you Need to Do Differently?
<--- Score

62. How do you select, collect, align, and integrate Performance testing data and information for tracking daily operations and overall organizational performance, including progress relative to strategic objectives and action plans?
<--- Score

63. Can support from partners be adjusted?
<--- Score

64. What are the known security controls?
<--- Score

65. How is change control managed?
<--- Score

66. Is there a dedicated performance test environment available or planned for carrying out performance testing?
<--- Score

67. How will Performance testing decisions be made and monitored?
<--- Score

68. How do you monitor usage and cost?
<--- Score

69. How do you plan on providing proper recognition and disclosure of supporting companies?
<--- Score

70. Who will be in control?
<--- Score

71. Who sets the Performance testing standards?
<--- Score

72. How might the group capture best practices and lessons learned so as to leverage improvements?
<--- Score

73. Will the team be available to assist members in planning investigations?
<--- Score

74. Is there a Performance testing Communication plan covering who needs to get what information when?

<--- Score

75. What is the control/monitoring plan?
<--- Score

76. What other systems, operations, processes, and infrastructures (hiring practices, staffing, training, incentives/rewards, metrics/dashboards/scorecards, etc.) need updates, additions, changes, or deletions in order to facilitate knowledge transfer and improvements?
<--- Score

77. What are the critical parameters to watch?
<--- Score

78. How widespread is its use?
<--- Score

79. Is there an action plan in case of emergencies?
<--- Score

80. Will any special training be provided for results interpretation?
<--- Score

81. What should you measure to verify efficiency gains?
<--- Score

82. What is the best design framework for Performance testing organization now that, in a post industrial-age if the top-down, command and control model is no longer relevant?
<--- Score

83. How do your controls stack up?
<--- Score

84. Implementation Planning: is a pilot needed to test the changes before a full roll out occurs?
<--- Score

85. How likely is the current Performance testing plan to come in on schedule or on budget?
<--- Score

86. How will the day-to-day responsibilities for monitoring and continual improvement be transferred from the improvement team to the process owner?
<--- Score

87. Are documented procedures clear and easy to follow for the operators?
<--- Score

88. Who has control over resources?
<--- Score

89. Have new or revised work instructions resulted?
<--- Score

90. How do you spread information?
<--- Score

91. Will your goals reflect your program budget?
<--- Score

92. How will report readings be checked to effectively monitor performance?
<--- Score

93. How will input, process, and output variables be checked to detect for sub-optimal conditions?
<--- Score

94. Does Performance testing appropriately measure and monitor risk?
<--- Score

95. What key inputs and outputs are being measured on an ongoing basis?
<--- Score

96. Where do ideas that reach policy makers and planners as proposals for Performance testing strengthening and reform actually originate?
<--- Score

97. How do you plan for the cost of succession?
<--- Score

98. How will the process owner verify improvement in present and future sigma levels, process capabilities?
<--- Score

99. Do you monitor the effectiveness of your Performance testing activities?
<--- Score

Add up total points for this section:
_ _ _ _ _ = Total points for this section

Divided by: _ _ _ _ _ _ (number of
statements answered) = _ _ _ _ _ _
Average score for this section

Transfer your score to the Performance
testing Index at the beginning of the
Self-Assessment.

CRITERION #7: SUSTAIN:

INTENT: Retain the benefits.

In my belief, the answer to this question is clearly defined:

5 Strongly Agree

4 Agree

3 Neutral

2 Disagree

1 Strongly Disagree

1. Why is Performance testing important for you now?
<--- Score

2. What is the difference between performance testing and load testing?
<--- Score

3. If no one would ever find out about your accomplishments, how would you lead differently?
<--- Score

4. What are the top 3 things at the forefront of your Performance testing agendas for the next 3 years?
<--- Score

5. Is your strategy driving your strategy? Or is the way in which you allocate resources driving your strategy?
<--- Score

6. What must you excel at?
<--- Score

7. How do you foster the skills, knowledge, talents, attributes, and characteristics you want to have?
<--- Score

8. How can you become the company that would put you out of business?
<--- Score

9. Do you have an implicit bias for capital investments over people investments?
<--- Score

10. What goals did you miss?
<--- Score

11. What are you challenging?
<--- Score

12. Who do you think the world wants your organization to be?
<--- Score

13. What is the kind of project structure that would be appropriate for your Performance testing project, should it be formal and complex, or can it be less

formal and relatively simple?
<--- Score

14. How do you keep records, of what?
<--- Score

15. What is the funding source for this project?
<--- Score

16. Did your employees make progress today?
<--- Score

17. What is your BATNA (best alternative to a negotiated agreement)?
<--- Score

18. Why should people listen to you?
<--- Score

19. Why is it important to have senior management support for a Performance testing project?
<--- Score

20. What is something you believe that nearly no one agrees with you on?
<--- Score

21. Where can you break convention?
<--- Score

22. Has implementation been effective in reaching specified objectives so far?
<--- Score

23. Whom among your colleagues do you trust, and for what?

<--- Score

24. Are you satisfied with your current role? If not, what is missing from it?
<--- Score

25. What is the source of the strategies for Performance testing strengthening and reform?
<--- Score

26. Are you relevant? Will you be relevant five years from now? Ten?
<--- Score

27. Are your responses positive or negative?
<--- Score

28. How do you accomplish your long range Performance testing goals?
<--- Score

29. Is your basic point _____ or _____?
<--- Score

30. Is it economical; do you have the time and money?
<--- Score

31. What are the success criteria that will indicate that Performance testing objectives have been met and the benefits delivered?
<--- Score

32. How do you know if you are successful?
<--- Score

33. How does Performance testing integrate with

other stakeholder initiatives?
<--- Score

34. Who do you want your customers to become?
<--- Score

35. Is the impact that Performance testing has shown?
<--- Score

36. Which individuals, teams or departments will be involved in Performance testing?
<--- Score

37. How do you lead with Performance testing in mind?
<--- Score

38. Which models, tools and techniques are necessary?
<--- Score

39. What are internal and external Performance testing relations?
<--- Score

40. Are all key stakeholders present at all Structured Walkthroughs?
<--- Score

41. Who will determine interim and final deadlines?
<--- Score

42. At what moment would you think; Will I get fired?
<--- Score

43. How do you listen to customers to obtain

actionable information?
<--- Score

44. How do you keep the momentum going?
<--- Score

45. How do you transition from the baseline to the target?
<--- Score

46. What do we do when new problems arise?
<--- Score

47. How do you cross-sell and up-sell your Performance testing success?
<--- Score

48. How do you maintain Performance testing's Integrity?
<--- Score

49. How do you ensure that implementations of Performance testing products are done in a way that ensures safety?
<--- Score

50. Who have you, as a company, historically been when you've been at your best?
<--- Score

51. Marketing budgets are tighter, consumers are more skeptical, and social media has changed forever the way we talk about Performance testing, how do you gain traction?
<--- Score

52. Would you rather sell to knowledgeable and informed customers or to uninformed customers?
<--- Score

53. How can you become more high-tech but still be high touch?
<--- Score

54. Is a Performance testing breakthrough on the horizon?
<--- Score

55. What are you trying to prove to yourself, and how might it be hijacking your life and business success?
<--- Score

56. What are the usability implications of Performance testing actions?
<--- Score

57. Who is responsible for errors?
<--- Score

58. What is an unauthorized commitment?
<--- Score

59. Who will manage the integration of tools?
<--- Score

60. Which Performance testing goals are the most important?
<--- Score

61. What is a feasible sequencing of reform initiatives over time?
<--- Score

62. What would have to be true for the option on the table to be the best possible choice?
<--- Score

63. What are your personal philosophies regarding Performance testing and how do they influence your work?
<--- Score

64. Do you think you know, or do you know you know ?
<--- Score

65. Do you have the right people on the bus?
<--- Score

66. If your company went out of business tomorrow, would anyone who doesn't get a paycheck here care?
<--- Score

67. Who, on the executive team or the board, has spoken to a customer recently?
<--- Score

68. Is a Performance testing team work effort in place?
<--- Score

69. Is there any existing Performance testing governance structure?
<--- Score

70. How do you set Performance testing stretch targets and how do you get people to not only participate in setting these stretch targets but also that they strive to achieve these?

<--- Score

71. In retrospect, of the projects that you pulled the plug on, what percent do you wish had been allowed to keep going, and what percent do you wish had ended earlier?
<--- Score

72. What counts that you are not counting?
<--- Score

73. Do you say no to customers for no reason?
<--- Score

74. What have been your experiences in defining long range Performance testing goals?
<--- Score

75. What is the range of capabilities?
<--- Score

76. If your customer were your grandmother, would you tell her to buy what you're selling?
<--- Score

77. Do you have the right capabilities and capacities?
<--- Score

78. What potential megatrends could make your business model obsolete?
<--- Score

79. What trophy do you want on your mantle?
<--- Score

80. How do you deal with Performance testing

changes?
<--- Score

81. What are the gaps in your knowledge and experience?
<--- Score

82. Is the performance testing program active and effective?
<--- Score

83. What are the key enablers to make this Performance testing move?
<--- Score

84. What happens at your organization when people fail?
<--- Score

85. Are you / should you be revolutionary or evolutionary?
<--- Score

86. How do you govern and fulfill your societal responsibilities?
<--- Score

87. Can you maintain your growth without detracting from the factors that have contributed to your success?
<--- Score

88. Is Performance testing dependent on the successful delivery of a current project?
<--- Score

89. What is the big Performance testing idea?
<--- Score

90. Who are your customers?
<--- Score

91. What is the recommended frequency of auditing?
<--- Score

92. What is your formula for success in Performance testing ?
<--- Score

93. How do you engage the workforce, in addition to satisfying them?
<--- Score

94. Is maximizing Performance testing protection the same as minimizing Performance testing loss?
<--- Score

95. How long will it take to change?
<--- Score

96. Are there any activities that you can take off your to do list?
<--- Score

97. What unique value proposition (UVP) do you offer?
<--- Score

98. Whose voice (department, ethnic group, women, older workers, etc) might you have missed hearing from in your company, and how might you amplify this voice to create positive momentum for your business?

<--- Score

99. What are the rules and assumptions your industry operates under? What if the opposite were true?
<--- Score

100. What new services of functionality will be implemented next with Performance testing ?
<--- Score

101. What are the essentials of internal Performance testing management?
<--- Score

102. Who will provide the final approval of Performance testing deliverables?
<--- Score

103. Who else should you help?
<--- Score

104. What management system can you use to leverage the Performance testing experience, ideas, and concerns of the people closest to the work to be done?
<--- Score

105. Are the criteria for selecting recommendations stated?
<--- Score

106. What is effective Performance testing?
<--- Score

107. What are strategies for increasing support and reducing opposition?

<--- Score

108. Are new benefits received and understood?
<--- Score

109. Will it be accepted by users?
<--- Score

110. When information truly is ubiquitous, when reach and connectivity are completely global, when computing resources are infinite, and when a whole new set of impossibilities are not only possible, but happening, what will that do to your business?
<--- Score

111. To whom do you add value?
<--- Score

112. What is your Performance testing strategy?
<--- Score

113. What relationships among Performance testing trends do you perceive?
<--- Score

114. If you had to rebuild your organization without any traditional competitive advantages (i.e., no killer technology, promising research, innovative product/ service delivery model, etcetera), how would your people have to approach their work and collaborate together in order to create the necessary conditions for success?
<--- Score

115. What business benefits will Performance testing goals deliver if achieved?

<--- Score

116. What current systems have to be understood and/or changed?
<--- Score

117. Will there be any necessary staff changes (redundancies or new hires)?
<--- Score

118. How will you insure seamless interoperability of Performance testing moving forward?
<--- Score

119. Have benefits been optimized with all key stakeholders?
<--- Score

120. Do Performance testing rules make a reasonable demand on a users capabilities?
<--- Score

121. What knowledge, skills and characteristics mark a good Performance testing project manager?
<--- Score

122. If you got fired and a new hire took your place, what would she do different?
<--- Score

123. How do you track customer value, profitability or financial return, organizational success, and sustainability?
<--- Score

124. How likely is it that a customer would

recommend your company to a friend or colleague?
<--- Score

125. If you find that you havent accomplished one of the goals for one of the steps of the Performance testing strategy, what will you do to fix it?
<--- Score

126. What are current Performance testing paradigms?
<--- Score

127. Why not do Performance testing?
<--- Score

128. What are the challenges?
<--- Score

129. What information is critical to your organization that your executives are ignoring?
<--- Score

130. What threat is Performance testing addressing?
<--- Score

131. What may be the consequences for the performance of an organization if all stakeholders are not consulted regarding Performance testing?
<--- Score

132. What is your performance testing?
<--- Score

133. What Performance testing modifications can you make work for you?
<--- Score

134. Do you see more potential in people than they do in themselves?
<--- Score

135. Why will customers want to buy your organizations products/services?
<--- Score

136. Is Performance testing realistic, or are you setting yourself up for failure?
<--- Score

137. Who are four people whose careers you have enhanced?
<--- Score

138. If you weren't already in this business, would you enter it today? And if not, what are you going to do about it?
<--- Score

139. What stupid rule would you most like to kill?
<--- Score

140. How do you make it meaningful in connecting Performance testing with what users do day-to-day?
<--- Score

141. Do you feel that more should be done in the Performance testing area?
<--- Score

142. Who uses your product in ways you never expected?
<--- Score

143. Who is responsible for ensuring appropriate resources (time, people and money) are allocated to Performance testing?
<--- Score

144. What is the overall business strategy?
<--- Score

145. How do you assess the Performance testing pitfalls that are inherent in implementing it?
<--- Score

146. How will you ensure you get what you expected?
<--- Score

147. What one word do you want to own in the minds of your customers, employees, and partners?
<--- Score

148. What are the short and long-term Performance testing goals?
<--- Score

149. What would you recommend your friend do if he/she were facing this dilemma?
<--- Score

150. Who will be responsible for deciding whether Performance testing goes ahead or not after the initial investigations?
<--- Score

151. How do you proactively clarify deliverables and Performance testing quality expectations?
<--- Score

152. If you had to leave your organization for a year and the only communication you could have with employees/colleagues was a single paragraph, what would you write?
<--- Score

153. Who do we want your customers to become?
<--- Score

154. How do senior leaders deploy your organizations vision and values through your leadership system, to the workforce, to key suppliers and partners, and to customers and other stakeholders, as appropriate?
<--- Score

155. What is the overall talent health of your organization as a whole at senior levels, and for each organization reporting to a member of the Senior Leadership Team?
<--- Score

156. What should you stop doing?
<--- Score

157. Do you know who is a friend or a foe?
<--- Score

158. How can you negotiate Performance testing successfully with a stubborn boss, an irate client, or a deceitful coworker?
<--- Score

159. Do you know what you are doing? And who do you call if you don't?
<--- Score

160. How do you go about securing Performance testing?
<--- Score

161. Who are the key stakeholders?
<--- Score

162. If you do not follow, then how to lead?
<--- Score

163. What are the business goals Performance testing is aiming to achieve?
<--- Score

164. Do you have enough freaky customers in your portfolio pushing you to the limit day in and day out?
<--- Score

165. Instead of going to current contacts for new ideas, what if you reconnected with dormant contacts--the people you used to know? If you were going reactivate a dormant tie, who would it be?
<--- Score

166. Can you do all this work?
<--- Score

167. What are the parameters of performance testing?
<--- Score

168. What Performance testing skills are most important?
<--- Score

169. What are the desirable features of an automatic performance testing tool for 3D applications?
<--- Score

170. What are the barriers to increased Performance testing production?
<--- Score

171. Is the Performance testing organization completing tasks effectively and efficiently?
<--- Score

172. What trouble can you get into?
<--- Score

173. If you were responsible for initiating and implementing major changes in your organization, what steps might you take to ensure acceptance of those changes?
<--- Score

174. In the past year, what have you done (or could you have done) to increase the accurate perception of your company/brand as ethical and honest?
<--- Score

175. How do you create buy-in?
<--- Score

176. Which functions and people interact with the supplier and or customer?
<--- Score

177. How much contingency will be available in the budget?

<--- Score

178. What are the potential basics of Performance testing fraud?
<--- Score

179. What was the last experiment you ran?
<--- Score

180. How will you motivate the stakeholders with the least vested interest?
<--- Score

181. Do you think Performance testing accomplishes the goals you expect it to accomplish?
<--- Score

182. What have you done to protect your business from competitive encroachment?
<--- Score

183. What happens if you do not have enough funding?
<--- Score

184. Is there a work around that you can use?
<--- Score

185. What role does communication play in the success or failure of a Performance testing project?
<--- Score

186. How important is Performance testing to the user organizations mission?
<--- Score

187. Who is the main stakeholder, with ultimate responsibility for driving Performance testing forward?
<--- Score

188. What are the metrics recommended for 3D performance testing?
<--- Score

189. Were lessons learned captured and communicated?
<--- Score

190. How do customers see your organization?
<--- Score

191. How are you doing compared to your industry?
<--- Score

192. Are assumptions made in Performance testing stated explicitly?
<--- Score

193. How can you incorporate support to ensure safe and effective use of Performance testing into the services that you provide?
<--- Score

194. What is the purpose of Performance testing in relation to the mission?
<--- Score

195. Are you changing as fast as the world around you?
<--- Score

196. How is implementation research currently incorporated into each of your goals?
<--- Score

197. What did you miss in the interview for the worst hire you ever made?
<--- Score

198. What is your competitive advantage?
<--- Score

199. What are the long-term Performance testing goals?
<--- Score

200. What could happen if you do not do it?
<--- Score

201. Ask yourself: how would you do this work if you only had one staff member to do it?
<--- Score

202. How much does Performance testing help?
<--- Score

203. How do you provide a safe environment -physically and emotionally?
<--- Score

204. Have new benefits been realized?
<--- Score

205. What is the estimated value of the project?
<--- Score

206. Do you have past Performance testing successes?

<--- Score

207. Why do and why don't your customers like your organization?
<--- Score

208. Can you break it down?
<--- Score

209. What is it like to work for you?
<--- Score

210. Are you using a design thinking approach and integrating Innovation, Performance testing Experience, and Brand Value?
<--- Score

211. Are the assumptions believable and achievable?
<--- Score

212. What are your most important goals for the strategic Performance testing objectives?
<--- Score

213. Who is on the team?
<--- Score

214. What you are going to do to affect the numbers?
<--- Score

215. What are specific Performance testing rules to follow?
<--- Score

216. Does the laboratory regularly participate successfully in a formal performance testing

system for the test methods in question?
<--- Score

217. If there were zero limitations, what would you do differently?
<--- Score

218. Can the schedule be done in the given time?
<--- Score

219. How do you manage Performance testing Knowledge Management (KM)?
<--- Score

220. How do you foster innovation?
<--- Score

221. Are you paying enough attention to the partners your company depends on to succeed?
<--- Score

222. How will you know that the Performance testing project has been successful?
<--- Score

223. What is your question? Why?
<--- Score

224. What happens when a new employee joins the organization?
<--- Score

225. How do you stay inspired?
<--- Score

226. What is the craziest thing you can do?

<--- Score

227. Political -is anyone trying to undermine this project?
<--- Score

228. Who is responsible for Performance testing?
<--- Score

229. In a project to restructure Performance testing outcomes, which stakeholders would you involve?
<--- Score

230. What will be the consequences to the stakeholder (financial, reputation etc) if Performance testing does not go ahead or fails to deliver the objectives?
<--- Score

231. Think of your Performance testing project, what are the main functions?
<--- Score

232. Why should you adopt a Performance testing framework?
<--- Score

233. How do you determine the key elements that affect Performance testing workforce satisfaction, how are these elements determined for different workforce groups and segments?
<--- Score

234. What projects are going on in the organization today, and what resources are those projects using from the resource pools?

<--- Score

235. Is there any reason to believe the opposite of my current belief?
<--- Score

236. Operational - will it work?
<--- Score

237. What does your signature ensure?
<--- Score

238. Are you maintaining a past–present–future perspective throughout the Performance testing discussion?
<--- Score

239. Are you making progress, and are you making progress as Performance testing leaders?
<--- Score

Add up total points for this section:
_ _ _ _ _ = Total points for this section

Divided by: _ _ _ _ _ _ (number of statements answered) = _ _ _ _ _ _
Average score for this section

Transfer your score to the Performance testing Index at the beginning of the Self-Assessment.

Performance testing and Managing Projects, Criteria for Project Managers:

1.0 Initiating Process Group: Performance testing

1. At which stage, in a typical Performance testing project do stake holders have maximum influence?

2. Were sponsors and decision makers available when needed outside regularly scheduled meetings?

3. Were resources available as planned?

4. Where must it be done?

5. What are the overarching issues of your organization?

6. How well did the chosen processes produce the expected results?

7. Do you know all the stakeholders impacted by the Performance testing project and what needs are?

8. Although the Performance testing project manager does not directly manage procurement and contracting activities, who does manage procurement and contracting activities in your organization then if not the PM?

9. Establishment of pm office?

10. How well did the chosen processes fit the needs of the Performance testing project?

11. Who is performing the work of the Performance testing project?

12. If action is called for, what form should it take?

13. When will the Performance testing project be done?

14. Based on your Performance testing project communication management plan, what worked well?

15. What communication items need improvement?

16. Did the Performance testing project team have the right skills?

17. Do you understand the quality and control criteria that must be achieved for successful Performance testing project completion?

18. How can you make your needs known?

19. For technology Performance testing projects only: Are all production support stakeholders (Business unit, technical support, & user) prepared for implementation with appropriate contingency plans?

20. What are the inputs required to produce the deliverables?

1.1 Project Charter: Performance testing

21. Dependent Performance testing projects: what Performance testing projects must be underway or completed before this Performance testing project can be successful?

22. What metrics could you look at?

23. Performance testing project objective statement: what must the Performance testing project do?

24. Why is a Performance testing project Charter used?

25. Where does all this information come from?

26. Major high-level milestone targets: what events measure progress?

27. How are Performance testing projects different from operations?

28. What is the business need?

29. When is a charter needed?

30. Why use a Performance testing project charter?

31. What barriers do you predict to your success?

32. What material?

33. Who will take notes, document decisions?

34. Is time of the essence?

35. What are some examples of a business case?

36. What are the assumptions?

37. Customer benefits: what customer requirements does this Performance testing project address?

38. What is the purpose of the Performance testing project?

39. What does it need to do?

40. Environmental stewardship and sustainability considerations: what is the process that will be used to ensure compliance with the environmental stewardship policy?

1.2 Stakeholder Register: Performance testing

41. What & Why?

42. How much influence do they have on the Performance testing project?

43. Who is managing stakeholder engagement?

44. What opportunities exist to provide communications?

45. Is your organization ready for change?

46. What is the power of the stakeholder?

47. How should employers make voices heard?

48. Who wants to talk about Security?

49. Who are the stakeholders?

50. How big is the gap?

51. How will reports be created?

52. What are the major Performance testing project milestones requiring communications or providing communications opportunities?

1.3 Stakeholder Analysis Matrix: Performance testing

53. Industry or lifestyle trends?

54. Where are the good opportunities facing your organizations development?

55. Is changing technology threatening your organizations position?

56. What do your organizations stakeholders do better than anyone else?

57. Guiding question: who shall you involve in the making of the stakeholder map?

58. Competitive advantages?

59. Who is most interested in information about the topic and/or has previously initiated interest?

60. What do you need to appraise?

61. Participatory approach: how will key stakeholders participate in the Performance testing project?

62. Why involve the stakeholder?

63. Usps (unique selling points)?

64. It developments?

65. What do you Evaluate?

66. Location and geographical?

67. What is the stakeholders name, what is function?

68. What are the mechanisms of public and social accountability, and how can they be made better?

69. Arena: in what fields are the actors active, where are they present?

70. Who will be affected by the work?

71. Is there a clear description of the scope of practice of the Performance testing projects educators?

72. How can you counter negative efforts?

2.0 Planning Process Group: Performance testing

73. Mitigate. what will you do to minimize the impact should a risk event occur?

74. Does the program have follow-up mechanisms (to verify the quality of the products, punctuality of delivery, etc.) to measure progress in the achievement of the envisaged results?

75. What is the difference between the early schedule and late schedule?

76. What is a Software Development Life Cycle (SDLC)?

77. To what extent is the program helping to influence your organizations policy framework?

78. If a task is partitionable, is this a sufficient condition to reduce the Performance testing project duration?

79. If a risk event occurs, what will you do?

80. Just how important is your work to the overall success of the Performance testing project?

81. How well do the team follow the chosen processes?

82. What do you need to do?

83. Professionals want to know what is expected from them; what are the deliverables?

84. How do you integrate Performance testing project Planning with the Iterative/Evolutionary SDLC?

85. Is the Performance testing project making progress in helping to achieve the set results?

86. What type of estimation method are you using?

87. Did you read it correctly?

88. In what way has the program contributed towards the issue culture and development included on the public agenda?

89. To what extent are the visions and actions of the partners consistent or divergent with regard to the program?

90. To what extent has a PMO contributed to raising the quality of the design of the Performance testing project?

91. When developing the estimates for Performance testing project phases, you choose to add the individual estimates for the activities that comprise each phase. What type of estimation method are you using?

2.1 Project Management Plan: Performance testing

92. Is the appropriate plan selected based on your organizations objectives and evaluation criteria expressed in Principles and Guidelines policies?

93. Who is the Performance testing project Manager?

94. What went wrong?

95. Are alternatives safe, functional, constructible, economical, reasonable and sustainable?

96. Will you add a schedule and diagram?

97. Is mitigation authorized or recommended?

98. Does the implementation plan have an appropriate division of responsibilities?

99. Are calculations and results of analyzes essentially correct?

100. What are the assigned resources?

101. What is the justification?

102. Why do you manage integration?

103. When is a Performance testing project management plan created?

104. Is the budget realistic?

105. Are the existing and future without-plan conditions reasonable and appropriate?

106. Has the selected plan been formulated using cost effectiveness and incremental analysis techniques?

107. What are the deliverables?

108. Does the selected plan protect privacy?

109. What should you drop in order to add something new?

110. Are the proposed Performance testing project purposes different than a previously authorized Performance testing project?

2.2 Scope Management Plan: Performance testing

111. Pop quiz – what changed on Performance testing project scope statement input?

112. Is the communication plan being followed?

113. Are corrective actions and variances reported?

114. Organizational unit (e.g., department, team, or person) who will accept responsibility for satisfactory completion of the item?

115. Does the title convey to the reader the essence of the Performance testing project?

116. Are software metrics formally captured, analyzed and used as a basis for other Performance testing project estimates?

117. Knowing the health of the Performance testing project – What is the status?

118. Are multiple estimation methods being employed?

119. Is stakeholder involvement adequate?

120. Describe how the deliverables will be verified against the Performance testing project scope. To whom will the deliverables be first presented for inspection and verification?

121. Have the key functions and capabilities been defined and assigned to each release or iteration?

122. Is the steering committee active in Performance testing project oversight?

123. Is there an on-going process in place to monitor Performance testing project risks?

124. Is each item clearly and completely defined?

125. How do you know how you are doing?

126. Have the procedures for identifying variances from estimates & adjusting the detailed work program been followed?

127. Has a Performance testing project Communications Plan been developed?

128. Is there a Steering Committee in place?

129. Are risk triggers captured?

2.3 Requirements Management Plan: Performance testing

130. Who came up with this requirement?

131. Who will finally present the work or product(s) for acceptance?

132. Is it new or replacing an existing business system or process?

133. Did you use declarative statements?

134. Who will approve the requirements (and if multiple approvers, in what order)?

135. How will unresolved questions be handled once approval has been obtained?

136. Is infrastructure setup part of your Performance testing project?

137. How will the information be distributed?

138. Are actual resources expenditures versus planned expenditures acceptable?

139. The wbs is developed as part of a joint planning session. and how do you know that youhave done this right?

140. Will you use an assessment of the Performance testing project environment as a tool to discover risk

to the requirements process?

141. Which hardware or software, related to, or as outcome of the Performance testing project is new to your organization?

142. Is the change control process documented?

143. Will you use tracing to help understand the impact of a change in requirements?

144. What performance metrics will be used?

145. Is the system software (non-operating system) new to the IT Performance testing project team?

146. Are all the stakeholders ready for the transition into the user community?

147. Is the user satisfied?

148. How will you communicate scheduled tasks to other team members?

149. What cost metrics will be used?

2.4 Requirements Documentation: Performance testing

150. Does your organization restrict technical alternatives?

151. Who is involved?

152. Are there any requirements conflicts?

153. Validity. does the system provide the functions which best support the customers needs?

154. Can you check system requirements?

155. How linear / iterative is your Requirements Gathering process (or will it be)?

156. What happens when requirements are wrong?

157. How does the proposed Performance testing project contribute to the overall objectives of your organization?

158. Has requirements gathering uncovered information that would necessitate changes?

159. How do you know when a Requirement is accurate enough?

160. Verifiability. can the requirements be checked?

161. What are current process problems?

162. What if the system wasn t implemented?

163. What images does it conjure?

164. Is the origin of the requirement clearly stated?

165. Who is interacting with the system?

166. Completeness. are all functions required by the customer included?

167. How do you get the user to tell you what they want?

168. What is your Elevator Speech?

169. How does what is being described meet the business need?

2.5 Requirements Traceability Matrix: Performance testing

170. Will you use a Requirements Traceability Matrix?

171. Why use a WBS?

172. How will it affect the stakeholders personally in career?

173. What are the chronologies, contingencies, consequences, criteria?

174. Why do you manage scope?

175. What is the WBS?

176. Do you have a clear understanding of all subcontracts in place?

177. Is there a requirements traceability process in place?

178. What percentage of Performance testing projects are producing traceability matrices between requirements and other work products?

179. How small is small enough?

180. How do you manage scope?

181. Describe the process for approving requirements so they can be added to the traceability matrix and

Performance testing project work can be performed. Will the Performance testing project requirements become approved in writing?

2.6 Project Scope Statement: Performance testing

182. Are the meetings set up to have assigned note takers that will add action/issues to the issue list?

183. Will all tasks resulting from issues be entered into the Performance testing project Plan and tracked through the plan?

184. Have you been able to easily identify success criteria and create objective measurements for each of the Performance testing project scopes goal statements?

185. Will tasks be marked complete only after QA has been successfully completed?

186. Has everyone approved the Performance testing projects scope statement?

187. Has a method and process for requirement tracking been developed?

188. Are there completion/verification criteria defined for each task producing an output?

189. Is an issue management process documented and filed?

190. Write a brief purpose statement for this Performance testing project. Include a business justification statement. What is the product of this

Performance testing project?

191. Is the plan under configuration management?

192. Elements of scope management that deal with concept development ?

193. Were potential customers involved early in the planning process?

194. Identify how your team and you will create the Performance testing project scope statement and the work breakdown structure (WBS). Document how you will create the Performance testing project scope statement and WBS, and make sure you answer the following questions: In defining Performance testing project scope and the WBS, will you and your Performance testing project team be using methods defined by your organization, methods defined by the Performance testing project management office (PMO), or other methods?

195. Will the Performance testing project risks be managed according to the Performance testing projects risk management process?

196. If there are vendors, have they signed off on the Performance testing project Plan?

197. Elements that deal with providing the detail?

198. Are there issues that could affect the existing requirements for the result, service, or product if the scope changes?

199. What is change?

200. Will the risk plan be updated on a regular and frequent basis?

2.7 Assumption and Constraint Log: Performance testing

201. Is this process still needed?

202. Would known impacts serve as impediments?

203. Does the document/deliverable meet all requirements (for example, statement of work) specific to this deliverable?

204. If appropriate, is the deliverable content consistent with current Performance testing project documents and in compliance with the Document Management Plan?

205. Have Performance testing project management standards and procedures been established and documented?

206. What do you log?

207. Does the plan conform to standards?

208. Are there nonconformance issues?

209. Is the steering committee active in Performance testing project oversight?

210. Are there processes defining how software will be developed including development methods, overall timeline for development, software product standards, and traceability?

211. How do you design an auditing system?

212. Violation trace: why ?

213. How can you prevent/fix violations?

214. Do the requirements meet the standards of correctness, completeness, consistency, accuracy, and readability?

215. What is positive about the current process?

216. Are there procedures in place to effectively manage interdependencies with other Performance testing projects / systems?

217. How many Performance testing project staff does this specific process affect?

218. Is the process working, and people are not executing in compliance of the process?

219. How relevant is this attribute to this Performance testing project or audit?

220. What worked well?

2.8 Work Breakdown Structure: Performance testing

221. When does it have to be done?

222. What has to be done?

223. What is the probability of completing the Performance testing project in less that xx days?

224. Why would you develop a Work Breakdown Structure?

225. How big is a work-package?

226. Is it still viable?

227. How far down?

228. Can you make it?

229. Who has to do it?

230. How much detail?

231. How will you and your Performance testing project team define the Performance testing projects scope and work breakdown structure?

232. Is it a change in scope?

233. When would you develop a Work Breakdown Structure?

234. Do you need another level?

235. How many levels?

236. When do you stop?

237. Where does it take place?

2.9 WBS Dictionary: Performance testing

238. Contemplated overhead expenditure for each period based on the best information currently available?

239. Are budgets or values assigned to work packages and planning packages in terms of dollars, hours, or other measurable units?

240. Are data elements summarized through the functional organizational structure for progressively higher levels of management?

241. Is authorization of budgets in excess of the contract budget base controlled formally and done with the full knowledge and recognition of the procuring activity?

242. Incurrence of actual indirect costs in excess of budgets, by element of expense?

243. Does the contractors system provide unit costs, equivalent unit or lot costs in terms of labor, material, other direct, and indirect costs?

244. Are retroactive changes to direct costs and indirect costs prohibited except for the correction of errors and routine accounting adjustments?

245. What is the goal?

246. Are your organizations and items of cost assigned to each pool identified?

247. Do procedures specify under what circumstances replanning of open work packages may occur, and the methods to be followed?

248. Time-phased control account budgets?

249. Are overhead costs budgets established on a basis consistent with anticipated direct business base?

250. Is all contract work included in the CWBS?

251. Are the requirements for all items of overhead established by rational, traceable processes?

252. What are you counting on?

253. The anticipated business volume?

254. What size should a work package be?

255. Software specification, development, integration, and testing, licenses ?

256. Are authorized changes being incorporated in a timely manner?

2.10 Schedule Management Plan: Performance testing

257. Are post milestone Performance testing project reviews (PMPR) conducted with your organization at least once a year?

258. Were stakeholders aware and supportive of the principles and practices of modern software estimation?

259. Have external dependencies been captured in the schedule?

260. Have adequate resources been provided by management to ensure Performance testing project success?

261. Is the schedule feasible and at what cost?

262. Has the scope management document been updated and distributed to help prevent scope creep?

263. Who is responsible for estimating the activity resources?

264. Who is responsible for estimating the activity durations?

265. Perform reality checks on schedules – are all tasks included?

266. Are all activities logically sequenced?

267. Sensitivity analysis?

268. Has a quality assurance plan been developed for the Performance testing project?

269. Pareto diagrams, statistical sampling, flow charting or trend analysis used quality monitoring?

270. Were the budget estimates reasonable?

271. Does the Performance testing project have a Quality Culture?

272. Is the plan consistent with industry best practices?

273. Have Performance testing project management standards and procedures been identified / established and documented?

274. Has the Performance testing project scope been baselined?

275. What does a valid Schedule look like?

276. Define units of measurement for each resource. For example, are you referencing gallons or liters?

2.11 Activity List: Performance testing

277. What is the total time required to complete the Performance testing project if no delays occur?

278. What will be performed?

279. Should you include sub-activities?

280. Can you determine the activity that must finish, before this activity can start?

281. How can the Performance testing project be displayed graphically to better visualize the activities?

282. What are the critical bottleneck activities?

283. How much slack is available in the Performance testing project?

284. How should ongoing costs be monitored to try to keep the Performance testing project within budget?

285. Is infrastructure setup part of your Performance testing project?

286. For other activities, how much delay can be tolerated?

287. Where will it be performed?

288. How do you determine the late start (LS) for each activity?

289. What went well?

290. How detailed should a Performance testing project get?

291. What is the probability the Performance testing project can be completed in xx weeks?

292. How will it be performed?

293. What is the LF and LS for each activity?

294. What went right?

295. In what sequence?

2.12 Activity Attributes: Performance testing

296. What is your organizations history in doing similar activities?

297. What activity do you think you should spend the most time on?

298. Time for overtime?

299. Resource is assigned to?

300. How difficult will it be to do specific activities on this Performance testing project?

301. What is missing?

302. Have constraints been applied to the start and finish milestones for the phases?

303. How do you manage time?

304. Has management defined a definite timeframe for the turnaround or Performance testing project window?

305. Are the required resources available?

306. How many resources do you need to complete the work scope within a limit of X number of days?

307. Were there other ways you could have organized

the data to achieve similar results?

308. Which method produces the more accurate cost assignment?

309. Resources to accomplish the work?

310. Have you identified the Activity Leveling Priority code value on each activity?

311. Activity: what is In the Bag?

312. How else could the items be grouped?

313. Can you re-assign any activities to another resource to resolve an over-allocation?

314. Why?

315. Where else does it apply?

2.13 Milestone List: Performance testing

316. Identify critical paths (one or more) and which activities are on the critical path?

317. How will the milestone be verified?

318. Which path is the critical path?

319. Describe the industry you are in and the market growth opportunities. What is the market for your technology, product or service?

320. Reliability of data, plan predictability?

321. Describe your organizations strengths and core competencies. What factors will make your organization succeed?

322. Continuity, supply chain robustness?

323. How late can the activity finish?

324. Do you foresee any technical risks or developmental challenges?

325. Vital contracts and partners?

326. How will you get the word out to customers?

327. When will the Performance testing project be complete?

328. What date will the task finish?

329. Marketing - reach, distribution, awareness?

330. Legislative effects?

331. How late can the activity start?

332. Sustainable financial backing?

333. New USPs?

2.14 Network Diagram: Performance testing

334. How confident can you be in your milestone dates and the delivery date?

335. What activities must occur simultaneously with this activity?

336. What job or jobs follow it?

337. What are the Key Success Factors?

338. How difficult will it be to do specific activities on this Performance testing project?

339. If the Performance testing project network diagram cannot change and you have extra personnel resources, what is the BEST thing to do?

340. What job or jobs could run concurrently?

341. If x is long, what would be the completion time if you break x into two parallel parts of y weeks and z weeks?

342. What job or jobs precede it?

343. What are the Major Administrative Issues?

344. Are the gantt chart and/or network diagram updated periodically and used to assess the overall Performance testing project timetable?

345. What are the tools?

346. What must be completed before an activity can be started?

347. Can you calculate the confidence level?

348. Exercise: what is the probability that the Performance testing project duration will exceed xx weeks?

349. What can be done concurrently?

350. What to do and When?

351. What is the probability of completing the Performance testing project in less that xx days?

352. What activities must follow this activity?

2.15 Activity Resource Requirements: Performance testing

353. What is the Work Plan Standard?

354. Do you use tools like decomposition and rolling-wave planning to produce the activity list and other outputs?

355. How do you handle petty cash?

356. How many signatures do you require on a check and does this match what is in your policy and procedures?

357. What are constraints that you might find during the Human Resource Planning process?

358. When does monitoring begin?

359. Anything else?

360. Which logical relationship does the PDM use most often?

361. Are there unresolved issues that need to be addressed?

362. Is there anything planned that does not need to be here?

363. Organizational Applicability?

364. Other support in specific areas?

365. Why do you do that?

2.16 Resource Breakdown Structure: Performance testing

366. How can this help you with team building?

367. When do they need the information?

368. What are the requirements for resource data?

369. What is the purpose of assigning and documenting responsibility?

370. What defines a successful Performance testing project?

371. Which resource planning tool provides information on resource responsibility and accountability?

372. Why do you do it?

373. Who will use the system?

374. What is the number one predictor of a groups productivity?

375. Why time management?

376. What is each stakeholders desired outcome for the Performance testing project?

377. Who will be used as a Performance testing project team member?

378. Who is allowed to see what data about which resources?

379. What can you do to improve productivity?

380. Who is allowed to perform which functions?

381. Is predictive resource analysis being done?

2.17 Activity Duration Estimates: Performance testing

382. Does a process exist to determine the potential loss or gain if risk events occur?

383. What are crucial elements of successful Performance testing project plan execution?

384. Will it help promote wellness at your organization and reduce insurance costs?

385. Is a work breakdown structure created to organize and to confirm the scope of each Performance testing project?

386. What is involved in the solicitation process?

387. How can others help Performance testing project managers understand your organizational context for Performance testing projects?

388. Is a formal written notice that the contract is complete provided to the seller?

389. Why is there a growing trend in outsourcing, especially in the government?

390. How can software assist in procuring goods and services?

391. What type of activity sequencing method is required for corresponding activities?

392. How can organizations use a weighted decision matrix to evaluate proposals as part of source selection?

393. Does a procedure exist to ensure the Performance testing project work is completed in the appropriate sequence and on time?

394. Are activity dependencies documented?

395. Which best describes the relationship between standard deviation and risk?

396. Have most organizations benefited from outsourcing?

397. How much time is required to develop it?

398. Which type of mathematical analysis is being used?

2.18 Duration Estimating Worksheet: Performance testing

399. What work will be included in the Performance testing project?

400. Is the Performance testing project responsive to community need?

401. How should ongoing costs be monitored to try to keep the Performance testing project within budget?

402. Science = process: remember the scientific method?

403. Done before proceeding with this activity or what can be done concurrently?

404. What questions do you have?

405. How can the Performance testing project be displayed graphically to better visualize the activities?

406. Can the Performance testing project be constructed as planned?

407. What info is needed?

408. Why estimate costs?

409. Will the Performance testing project collaborate with the local community and leverage resources?

410. Is this operation cost effective?

411. Small or large Performance testing project?

412. When does your organization expect to be able to complete it?

413. When do the individual activities need to start and finish?

414. Value pocket identification & quantification what are value pockets?

2.19 Project Schedule: Performance testing

415. How do you manage Performance testing project Risk?

416. What is the difference?

417. How detailed should a Performance testing project get?

418. If there are any qualifying green components to this Performance testing project, what portion of the total Performance testing project cost is green?

419. Why do you need to manage Performance testing project Risk?

420. How does a Performance testing project get to be a year late ?

421. How closely did the initial Performance testing project Schedule compare with the actual schedule?

422. How effectively were issues able to be resolved without impacting the Performance testing project Schedule or Budget?

423. How can slack be negative?

424. Are key risk mitigation strategies added to the Performance testing project schedule?

425. Performance testing project work estimates Who is managing the work estimate quality of work tasks in the Performance testing project schedule?

426. Did the final product meet or exceed user expectations?

427. What does that mean?

428. Why is software Performance testing project disaster so common?

429. Why do you need schedules?

430. What is risk?

2.20 Cost Management Plan: Performance testing

431. Is quality monitored from the perspective of the customers needs and expectations?

432. Is your organization certified as a supplier, wholesaler, regular dealer, or manufacturer of corresponding products/supplies?

433. Risk rating?

434. Schedule variances – how will schedule variances be identified and corrected?

435. Cost estimate preparation – What cost estimates will be prepared during the Performance testing project phases?

436. Are updated Performance testing project time & resource estimates reasonable based on the current Performance testing project stage?

437. Has the schedule been baselined?

438. Environmental management – what changes in statutory environmental compliance requirements are anticipated during the Performance testing project?

439. Is there general agreement & acceptance of the current status and progress of the Performance testing project?

440. Have all documents been archived in a Performance testing project repository for each release?

441. Is there an issues management plan in place?

442. Is there anything unique in this Performance testing projects scope statement that will affect resources?

443. Are all vendor contracts closed out?

444. What strengths do you have?

445. Owner, contractor, and subcontractors?

446. Contractors scope – how will contractors scope be defined when contracts are let?

447. Exclusions – is there scope to be performed or provided by others?

448. Performance testing project Objectives?

449. Does the detailed work plan match the complexity of tasks with the capabilities of personnel?

450. Have process improvement efforts been completed before requirements efforts begin?

2.21 Activity Cost Estimates: Performance testing

451. Are cost subtotals needed?

452. How do you change activities?

453. Where can you get activity reports?

454. Is there anything unique in this Performance testing projects scope statement that will affect resources?

455. Who & what determines the need for contracted services?

456. What is the activity inventory?

457. Does the estimator have experience?

458. Were you satisfied with the work?

459. Who determines the quality and expertise of contractors?

460. When do you enter into PPM?

461. How Award?

462. What are you looking for?

463. Why do you manage cost?

464. What is a Performance testing project Management Plan?

465. Eac -estimate at completion, what is the total job expected to cost?

466. Can you change your activities?

467. How difficult will it be to do specific tasks on the Performance testing project?

468. What happens if you cannot produce the documentation for the single audit?

469. Did the consultant work with local staff to develop local capacity?

2.22 Cost Estimating Worksheet: Performance testing

470. Who is best positioned to know and assist in identifying corresponding factors?

471. What is the purpose of estimating?

472. Is the Performance testing project responsive to community need?

473. What is the estimated labor cost today based upon this information?

474. Does the Performance testing project provide innovative ways for stakeholders to overcome obstacles or deliver better outcomes?

475. Is it feasible to establish a control group arrangement?

476. Will the Performance testing project collaborate with the local community and leverage resources?

477. How will the results be shared and to whom?

478. Ask: are others positioned to know, are others credible, and will others cooperate?

479. What will others want?

480. What costs are to be estimated?

481. What happens to any remaining funds not used?

482. What can be included?

483. Identify the timeframe necessary to monitor progress and collect data to determine how the selected measure has changed?

484. What additional Performance testing project(s) could be initiated as a result of this Performance testing project?

485. Can a trend be established from historical performance data on the selected measure and are the criteria for using trend analysis or forecasting methods met?

2.23 Cost Baseline: Performance testing

486. Is request in line with priorities?

487. How do you manage cost?

488. Has the appropriate access to relevant data and analysis capability been granted?

489. Have all approved changes to the cost baseline been identified and impact on the Performance testing project documented?

490. If you sold 10x widgets on a day, what would the affect on profits be?

491. Has the Performance testing project documentation been archived or otherwise disposed as described in the Performance testing project communication plan?

492. How likely is it to go wrong?

493. What is cost and Performance testing project cost management?

494. Where do changes come from?

495. Does the suggested change request seem to represent a necessary enhancement to the product?

496. Is the cr within Performance testing project

scope?

497. Does the suggested change request represent a desired enhancement to the products functionality?

498. Verify business objectives. Are others appropriate, and well-articulated?

499. Is there anything unique in this Performance testing projects scope statement that will affect resources?

500. Has the actual cost of the Performance testing project (or Performance testing project phase) been tallied and compared to the approved budget?

501. Does a process exist for establishing a cost baseline to measure Performance testing project performance?

502. Are you meeting with your team regularly?

503. Are there contingencies or conditions related to the acceptance?

2.24 Quality Management Plan: Performance testing

504. How are deviations from procedures handled?

505. How are people conducting sampling trained?

506. What other teams / processes would be impacted by changes to the current process, and how?

507. How do you ensure that your sampling methods and procedures meet your data quality objectives?

508. How is staff trained on the recording of field notes?

509. How are corresponding standards measured?

510. Does a prospective decision remain the same regardless of what the data show is?

511. Who is responsible for approving the qapp?

512. Were there any deficiencies / issues in prior years self-assessment?

513. How is equipment calibrated?

514. Who is responsible for writing the qapp?

515. Meet how often?

516. Can it be done better?

517. How does the material compare to a regulatory threshold?

518. How do you field-modify testing procedures?

519. Is there a Quality Management Plan?

520. Checking the completeness and appropriateness of the sampling and testing. Were the right locations/samples tested for the right parameters?

521. You know what your customers expectations are regarding this process?

522. Does the system design reflect the requirements?

523. What field records are generated?

2.25 Quality Metrics: Performance testing

524. What documentation is required?

525. Did evaluation start on time?

526. Are quality metrics defined?

527. Does risk analysis documentation meet standards?

528. Who notifies stakeholders of normal and abnormal results?

529. How effective are your security tests?

530. Who is willing to lead?

531. What are you trying to accomplish?

532. What level of statistical confidence do you use?

533. What is the benchmark?

534. How do you calculate such metrics?

535. How is it being measured?

536. Is there alignment within your organization on definitions?

537. Is there a set of procedures to capture, analyze

and act on quality metrics?

538. How should customers provide input?

539. Which report did you use to create the data you are submitting?

540. Where is quality now?

541. What is the CMS Benchmark?

542. Do you stratify metrics by product or site?

543. Which data do others need in one place to target areas of improvement?

2.26 Process Improvement Plan: Performance testing

544. Are there forms and procedures to collect and record the data?

545. Does explicit definition of the measures exist?

546. Why do you want to achieve the goal?

547. Who should prepare the process improvement action plan?

548. Modeling current processes is great, and will you ever see a return on that investment?

549. What actions are needed to address the problems and achieve the goals?

550. The motive is determined by asking, Why do you want to achieve this goal?

551. Are you meeting the quality standards?

552. What is the test-cycle concept?

553. What personnel are the change agents for your initiative?

554. Management commitment at all levels?

555. Where do you want to be?

556. Are you making progress on the goals?

557. What personnel are the champions for the initiative?

558. Does your process ensure quality?

559. Has the time line required to move measurement results from the points of collection to databases or users been established?

560. What lessons have you learned so far?

561. Where do you focus?

2.27 Responsibility Assignment Matrix: Performance testing

562. Does the contractors system identify work accomplishment against the schedule plan?

563. Is budgeted cost for work performed calculated in a manner consistent with the way work is planned?

564. Does the contractors system provide unit or lot costs when applicable?

565. Are people encouraged to bring up issues?

566. All cwbs elements specified for external reporting?

567. Performance testing projected economic escalation?

568. Past experience – the person or the group worked at something similar in the past?

569. Is cost and schedule performance measurement done in a consistent, systematic manner?

570. Do all the identified groups or people really need to be consulted?

571. Contract line items and end items?

572. Is the entire contract planned in time-phased control accounts to the extent practicable?

573. The already stated responsible for overhead performance control of related costs?

574. Budgets assigned to major functional organizations?

575. Is the anticipated (firm and potential) business base Performance testing projected in a rational, consistent manner?

576. Are the actual costs used for variance analysis reconcilable with data from the accounting system?

2.28 Roles and Responsibilities: Performance testing

577. Key conclusions and recommendations: Are conclusions and recommendations relevant and acceptable?

578. Required skills, knowledge, experience?

579. Are governance roles and responsibilities documented?

580. Be specific; avoid generalities. Thank you and great work alone are insufficient. What exactly do you appreciate and why?

581. What should you do now to ensure that you are meeting all expectations of your current position?

582. Once the responsibilities are defined for the Performance testing project, have the deliverables, roles and responsibilities been clearly communicated to every participant?

583. Is feedback clearly communicated and non-judgmental?

584. Was the expectation clearly communicated?

585. Where are you most strong as a supervisor?

586. Attainable / achievable: the goal is attainable; can you actually accomplish the goal?

587. Accountabilities: what are the roles and responsibilities of individual team members?

588. What is working well?

589. What areas of supervision are challenging for you?

590. What expectations were met?

591. Concern: where are you limited or have no authority, where you can not influence?

592. What should you highlight for improvement?

593. Are the quality assurance functions and related roles and responsibilities clearly defined?

594. What expectations were NOT met?

595. Are your budgets supportive of a culture of quality data?

2.29 Human Resource Management Plan: Performance testing

596. Have all documents been archived in a Performance testing project repository for each release?

597. Are all resource assumptions documented?

598. Specific - is the objective clear in terms of what, how, when, and where the situation will be changed?

599. Are the schedule estimates reasonable given the Performance testing project?

600. Are the Performance testing project plans updated on a frequent basis?

601. Measurable - are the targets measurable?

602. What did you have to assume to be true to complete the charter?

603. Is there a formal set of procedures supporting Issues Management?

604. Do Performance testing project managers participating in the Performance testing project know the Performance testing projects true status first hand?

605. Are people being developed to meet the challenges of the future?

606. Are software metrics formally captured, analyzed and used as a basis for other Performance testing project estimates?

607. Where is your organization headed?

608. Is there a formal set of procedures supporting Stakeholder Management?

609. Are the payment terms being followed?

610. Staffing Requirements?

611. Were Performance testing project team members involved in the development of activity & task decomposition?

2.30 Communications Management Plan: Performance testing

612. What communications method?

613. What steps can you take for a positive relationship?

614. Who is responsible?

615. Do you have members of your team responsible for certain stakeholders?

616. Who have you worked with in past, similar initiatives?

617. How will the person responsible for executing the communication item be notified?

618. What is the political influence?

619. Do you feel a register helps?

620. Are there common objectives between the team and the stakeholder?

621. What help do you and your team need from the stakeholder?

622. Are there potential barriers between the team and the stakeholder?

623. Which team member will work with each

stakeholder?

624. Is there an important stakeholder who is actively opposed and will not receive messages?

625. Who to share with?

626. Which stakeholders are thought leaders, influences, or early adopters?

627. What approaches do you use?

628. Are others needed?

629. What are the interrelationships?

630. What is the stakeholders level of authority?

631. Who is the stakeholder?

2.31 Risk Management Plan: Performance testing

632. Are the metrics meaningful and useful?

633. What would you do differently?

634. Is the customer willing to commit significant time to the requirements gathering process?

635. What is the probability the risk avoidance strategy will be successful?

636. What will the damage be?

637. Have you worked with the customer in the past?

638. How much risk can you tolerate?

639. Risk categories: what are the main categories of risks that should be addressed on this Performance testing project?

640. What is the cost to the Performance testing project if it does occur?

641. Are the best people available?

642. What does a risk management program do?

643. Market risk: will the new product be useful to your organization or marketable to others?

644. What things might go wrong?

645. If you can not fix it, how do you do it differently?

646. Have customers been involved fully in the definition of requirements?

647. Risk documentation: what reporting formats and processes will be used for risk management activities?

648. Risks should be identified during which phase of Performance testing project management life cycle?

649. Workarounds are determined during which step of risk management?

650. Management -what contingency plans do you have if the risk becomes a reality?

651. What will drive change?

2.32 Risk Register: Performance testing

652. What has changed since the last period?

653. What action, if any, has been taken to respond to the risk?

654. Methodology: how will risk management be performed on this Performance testing project?

655. What further options might be available for responding to the risk?

656. Technology risk -is the Performance testing project technically feasible?

657. When is it going to be done?

658. Budget and schedule: what are the estimated costs and schedules for performing risk-related activities?

659. Assume the event happens, what is the Most Likely impact?

660. What are the main aims, objectives of the policy, strategy, or service and the intended outcomes?

661. What is the reason for current performance gaps and do the risks and opportunities identified previously account for this?

662. What may happen or not go according to plan?

663. Have other controls and solutions been implemented in other services which could be applied as an alternative to additional funding?

664. What is the probability and impact of the risk occurring?

665. What should the audit role be in establishing a risk management process?

666. What will be done?

667. Recovery actions - planned actions taken once a risk has occurred to allow you to move on. What should you do after?

668. Manageability – have mitigations to the risk been identified?

669. Why would you develop a risk register?

670. When will it happen?

2.33 Probability and Impact Assessment: Performance testing

671. Are end-users enthusiastically committed to the Performance testing project and the system/product to be built?

672. When and how will the recent breakthroughs in basic research lead to commercial products?

673. What should be the level of difficulty in handling the technology?

674. What are the current demands of the customer?

675. What risks are necessary to achieve success?

676. What will be the impact or consequence if the risk occurs?

677. Is there additional information that would make you more confident about your analysis?

678. What risks does the employee encounter?

679. Assuming that you have identified a number of risks in the Performance testing project, how would you prioritize them?

680. What is the experience (performance, attitude, business ethics, etc.) in the past with contractors?

681. Does the customer understand the software

process?

682. Supply/demand Performance testing projections and trends; what are the levels of accuracy?

683. Is the customer technically sophisticated in the product area?

684. Costs associated with late delivery or a defective product?

685. Does the Performance testing project team have experience with the technology to be implemented?

686. What are its business ethics?

687. What are the channels available for distribution to the customer?

688. What are the current or emerging trends of culture?

689. What is the likelihood?

2.34 Probability and Impact Matrix: Performance testing

690. Do you use any methods to analyze risks?

691. How should you structure risks?

692. What is the industrial relations prevailing in this organization?

693. Brain storm – mind maps, what if?

694. Who is going to be the consortium leader?

695. Do requirements put excessive performance constraints on the product?

696. What are the preparations required for facing difficulties?

697. Have top software and customer managers formally committed to support the Performance testing project?

698. How realistic is the timing of introduction?

699. Can it be changed quickly?

700. Who are the owners?

701. What is your anticipated volatility of the requirements?

702. Are team members trained in the use of the tools?

703. Which of the risk factors can be avoided altogether?

704. Can the Performance testing project proceed without assuming the risk?

705. How solid is the Performance testing projection of competitive reaction?

706. What will be the environmental impact of the Performance testing project?

2.35 Risk Data Sheet: Performance testing

707. What is the environment within which you operate (social trends, economic, community values, broad based participation, national directions etc.)?

708. What are the main threats to your existence?

709. Is the data sufficiently specified in terms of the type of failure being analyzed, and its frequency or probability?

710. What are you here for (Mission)?

711. What is the chance that it will happen?

712. What can happen?

713. What can you do?

714. How can hazards be reduced?

715. What will be the consequences if the risk happens?

716. What will be the consequences if it happens?

717. Potential for recurrence?

718. What is the likelihood of it happening?

719. What do people affected think about the need

for, and practicality of preventive measures?

720. Risk of what?

721. Whom do you serve (customers)?

722. Who has a vested interest in how you perform as your organization (our stakeholders)?

723. Has a sensitivity analysis been carried out?

724. Type of risk identified?

725. Do effective diagnostic tests exist?

2.36 Procurement Management Plan: Performance testing

726. Is there a procurement management plan in place?

727. Are the quality tools and methods identified in the Quality Plan appropriate to the Performance testing project?

728. Is there any form of automated support for Issues Management?

729. Have the procedures for identifying budget variances been followed?

730. Are meeting minutes captured and sent out after meetings?

731. Are tasks tracked by hours?

732. Are procurement deliverables arriving on time and to specification?

733. Has the business need been clearly defined?

734. Has a resource management plan been created?

735. Has the Performance testing project manager been identified?

736. Has the Performance testing project scope been baselined?

737. Are there checklists created to determine if all quality processes are followed?

738. Are Performance testing project leaders committed to this Performance testing project full time?

739. Do Performance testing project managers participating in the Performance testing project know the Performance testing projects true status first hand?

740. Are parking lot items captured?

741. Is there an on-going process in place to monitor Performance testing project risks?

742. Do Performance testing project teams & team members report on status / activities / progress?

2.37 Source Selection Criteria: Performance testing

743. When and what information can be considered with offerors regarding past performance?

744. How do you ensure an integrated assessment of proposals?

745. What instructions should be provided regarding oral presentations?

746. How are oral presentations documented?

747. What is the role of counsel in the procurement process?

748. How are clarifications and communications appropriately used?

749. Are considerations anticipated?

750. Are there any specific considerations that precludes offers from being selected as the awardee?

751. Is the offeror pricing what is technically proposed?

752. When is it appropriate to issue a Draft Request for Proposal (DRFP)?

753. Are types/quantities of material, facilities appropriate?

754. What documentation is needed for a tradeoff decision?

755. What is the effect of the debriefing schedule on potential protests?

756. What should a Draft Request for Proposal (DRFP) include?

757. Can you reasonably estimate total organization requirements for the coming year?

758. What should a DRFP include?

759. Do you want to wait until all offerors have been evaluated?

760. How can solicitation Schedules be improved to yield more effective price competition?

761. Do you ensure you evaluate what you asked for, not what you want to see or expect to see?

762. What can not be disclosed?

2.38 Stakeholder Management Plan: Performance testing

763. Where will verification occur, and by whom?

764. Are the appropriate IT resources adequate to meet planned commitments?

765. What has to be purchased?

766. What are reporting requirements?

767. Was trending evident between audits?

768. How accurate and complete is the information?

769. What are the criteria for selecting suppliers of off the shelf products?

770. What is the process for purchases that arent acceptable (eg damaged goods)?

771. How is information analyzed, and what specific pieces of data would be of interest to the Performance testing project manager?

772. Why is it important to reduce deliverables to a smallest component?

773. Does the Performance testing project have a Quality Culture?

774. Is a pmo (Performance testing project

management office) in place and does it provide oversight to the Performance testing project?

775. Have reserves been created to address risks?

776. Have adequate resources been provided by management to ensure Performance testing project success?

777. Is staff trained on the software technologies that are being used on the Performance testing project?

778. Are the Performance testing project team members located locally to the users/stakeholders?

779. Are communication systems proposed compatible with staff skills and experience?

780. Are there cosmetic errors that hinder readability and comprehension?

2.39 Change Management Plan: Performance testing

781. How does the principle of senders and receivers make the Performance testing project communications effort more complex?

782. What risks may occur upfront?

783. How much Performance testing project management is needed?

784. What are the dependencies?

785. Do you need new systems?

786. Is it the same for each of the business units?

787. Who will do the training?

788. What type of materials/channels will be available to leverage?

789. Who might be able to help you the most?

790. What policies and procedures need to be changed?

791. Different application of an existing process?

792. Will all field readiness criteria have been practically met prior to training roll-out?

793. When should a given message be communicated?

794. Change invariability confront many relationships especially the already stated that require a set of behaviours What roles with in your organization are affected and how?

795. What are the specific target groups / audience that will be impacted by this change?

796. How frequently should you repeat the message?

797. Would you need to tailor a special message for each segment of the audience?

798. Impact of systems implementation on organization change?

799. Readiness -what is a successful end state?

3.0 Executing Process Group: Performance testing

800. Do your results resemble a normal distribution?

801. Is the schedule for the set products being met?

802. How could stakeholders negatively impact your Performance testing project?

803. What factors are contributing to progress or delay in the achievement of products and results?

804. Why should Performance testing project managers strive to make jobs look easy?

805. How is Performance testing project performance information created and distributed?

806. How can software assist in Performance testing project communications?

807. Based on your Performance testing project communication management plan, what worked well?

808. How do you prevent staff are just doing busywork to pass the time?

809. Who will provide training?

810. What is the product of your Performance testing project?

811. Will additional funds be needed for hardware or software?

812. When do you share the scorecard with managers?

813. It under budget or over budget?

814. What were things that you need to improve?

815. What is the shortest possible time it will take to complete this Performance testing project?

816. What is the difference between conceptual, application, and evaluative questions?

817. How does a Performance testing project life cycle differ from a product life cycle?

818. How could you control progress of your Performance testing project?

3.1 Team Member Status Report: Performance testing

819. Does the product, good, or service already exist within your organization?

820. How much risk is involved?

821. Are your organizations Performance testing projects more successful over time?

822. What specific interest groups do you have in place?

823. Do you have an Enterprise Performance testing project Management Office (EPMO)?

824. How can you make it practical?

825. Are the attitudes of staff regarding Performance testing project work improving?

826. Is there evidence that staff is taking a more professional approach toward management of your organizations Performance testing projects?

827. How it is to be done?

828. How will resource planning be done?

829. Does every department have to have a Performance testing project Manager on staff?

830. Why is it to be done?

831. When a teams productivity and success depend on collaboration and the efficient flow of information, what generally fails them?

832. The problem with Reward & Recognition Programs is that the truly deserving people all too often get left out. How can you make it practical?

833. Will the staff do training or is that done by a third party?

834. Are the products of your organizations Performance testing projects meeting customers objectives?

835. How does this product, good, or service meet the needs of the Performance testing project and your organization as a whole?

836. Does your organization have the means (staff, money, contract, etc.) to produce or to acquire the product, good, or service?

837. What is to be done?

3.2 Change Request: Performance testing

838. What are the requirements for urgent changes?

839. What can be filed?

840. What is the change request log?

841. When do you create a change request?

842. Why were your requested changes rejected or not made?

843. How do team members communicate with each other?

844. Will all change requests be unconditionally tracked through this process?

845. Who will perform the change?

846. How can you ensure that changes have been made properly?

847. How does your organization control changes before and after software is released to a customer?

848. Will there be a change request form in use?

849. What mechanism is used to appraise others of changes that are made?

850. How many times must the change be modified or presented to the change control board before it is approved?

851. Can static requirements change attributes like the size of the change be used to predict reliability in execution?

852. Is it feasible to use requirements attributes as predictors of reliability?

853. Are there requirements attributes that are strongly related to the occurrence of defects and failures?

854. Who is responsible for the implementation and monitoring of all measures?

855. How is quality being addressed on the Performance testing project?

856. Who needs to approve change requests?

857. Screen shots or attachments included in a Change Request?

3.3 Change Log: Performance testing

858. Is the requested change request a result of changes in other Performance testing project(s)?

859. Is this a mandatory replacement?

860. Will the Performance testing project fail if the change request is not executed?

861. Do the described changes impact on the integrity or security of the system?

862. When was the request submitted?

863. How does this change affect scope?

864. Who initiated the change request?

865. How does this change affect the timeline of the schedule?

866. Is the change backward compatible without limitations?

867. Is the submitted change a new change or a modification of a previously approved change?

868. When was the request approved?

869. Is the change request within Performance testing project scope?

870. How does this relate to the standards developed

for specific business processes?

871. Should a more thorough impact analysis be conducted?

872. Is the change request open, closed or pending?

3.4 Decision Log: Performance testing

873. How do you define success?

874. What alternatives/risks were considered?

875. How consolidated and comprehensive a story can you tell by capturing currently available incident data in a central location and through a log of key decisions during an incident?

876. Adversarial environment. is your opponent open to a non-traditional workflow, or will it likely challenge anything you do?

877. What are the cost implications?

878. With whom was the decision shared or considered?

879. Does anything need to be adjusted?

880. What was the rationale for the decision?

881. How does provision of information, both in terms of content and presentation, influence acceptance of alternative strategies?

882. How does an increasing emphasis on cost containment influence the strategies and tactics used?

883. Linked to original objective?

884. Behaviors; what are guidelines that the team has identified that will assist them with getting the most out of team meetings?

885. How do you know when you are achieving it?

886. It becomes critical to track and periodically revisit both operational effectiveness; Are you noticing all that you need to, and are you interpreting what you see effectively?

887. Is everything working as expected?

888. What eDiscovery problem or issue did your organization set out to fix or make better?

889. What is your overall strategy for quality control / quality assurance procedures?

890. Do strategies and tactics aimed at less than full control reduce the costs of management or simply shift the cost burden?

891. What is the line where eDiscovery ends and document review begins?

892. How does the use a Decision Support System influence the strategies/tactics or costs?

3.5 Quality Audit: Performance testing

893. Are there sufficient personnel having the necessary education, background, training, and experience to assure that all operations are correctly performed?

894. What mechanisms exist for identification of staff development needs?

895. How does your organization know that its range of activities are being reviewed as rigorously and constructively as they could be?

896. How well do you think your organization engages with the outside community?

897. How does your organization know that its risk management system is appropriately effective and constructive?

898. How does your organization know that the system for managing its facilities is appropriately effective and constructive?

899. How does your organization know that its relationships with other relevant organizations are appropriately effective and constructive?

900. How does your organization know that its quality of teaching is appropriately effective and constructive?

901. How are you auditing your organizations compliance with regulations?

902. How does your organization know that the support for its staff is appropriately effective and constructive?

903. What will the Observer get to Observe?

904. Are storage areas and reconditioning operations designed to prevent mix-ups and assure orderly handling of both the distressed and reconditioned devices?

905. How does your organization know that its relationship with its (past) staff is appropriately effective and constructive?

906. Are training programs documented?

907. What are your supplier audits?

908. How does your organization know that its promotions system is appropriately effective, constructive and fair?

909. How does your organization know that its system for managing intellectual property issues is appropriately effective, constructive and fair?

910. Is your organizations resource allocation system properly aligned with its collection of intentions?

911. How does your organization know that its system for attending to the health and wellbeing of its staff is

appropriately effective and constructive?

912. Are there appropriate indicators for monitoring the effectiveness and efficiency of processes?

3.6 Team Directory: Performance testing

913. Why is the work necessary?

914. Who will write the meeting minutes and distribute?

915. Timing: when do the effects of communication take place?

916. Decisions: what could be done better to improve the quality of the constructed product?

917. What are you going to deliver or accomplish?

918. Who should receive information (all stakeholders)?

919. Where should the information be distributed?

920. Process decisions: are all start-up, turn over and close out requirements of the contract satisfied?

921. How do unidentified risks impact the outcome of the Performance testing project?

922. What needs to be communicated?

923. How does the team resolve conflicts and ensure tasks are completed?

924. Decisions: is the most suitable form of contract

being used?

925. Contract requirements complied with?

926. When will you produce deliverables?

927. Who are the Team Members?

928. When does information need to be distributed?

929. Who will be the stakeholders on your next Performance testing project?

930. How will the team handle changes?

931. Where will the product be used and/or delivered or built when appropriate?

3.7 Team Operating Agreement: Performance testing

932. Why does your organization want to participate in teaming?

933. Do you use a parking lot for any items that are important and outside of the agenda?

934. Are there more than two national cultures represented by your team?

935. Did you draft the meeting agenda?

936. Do team members reside in more than two countries?

937. Do you call or email participants to ensure understanding, follow-through and commitment to the meeting outcomes?

938. Did you recap the meeting purpose, time, and expectations?

939. Do you post any action items, due dates, and responsibilities on the team website?

940. What are some potential sources of conflict among team members?

941. Must your team members rely on the expertise of other members to complete tasks?

942. Are team roles clearly defined and accepted?

943. Is compensation based on team and individual performance?

944. How will you divide work equitably?

945. What resources can be provided for the team in terms of equipment, space, time for training, protected time and space for meetings, and travel allowances?

946. How will your group handle planned absences?

947. How does teaming fit in with overall organizational goals and meet organizational needs?

948. Resource allocation: how will individual team members account for time and expenses, and how will this be allocated in the team budget?

949. Must your members collaborate successfully to complete Performance testing projects?

950. What are the boundaries (organizational or geographic) within which you operate?

951. Do you determine the meeting length and time of day?

3.8 Team Performance Assessment: Performance testing

952. Effects of crew composition on crew performance: Does the whole equal the sum of its parts?

953. To what degree does the teams work approach provide opportunity for members to engage in fact-based problem solving?

954. How do you manage human resources?

955. What makes opportunities more or less obvious?

956. To what degree will the team adopt a concrete, clearly understood, and agreed-upon approach that will result in achievement of the teams goals?

957. To what degree do all members feel responsible for all agreed-upon measures?

958. To what degree will the team ensure that all members equitably share the work essential to the success of the team?

959. To what degree does the teams purpose contain themes that are particularly meaningful and memorable?

960. To what degree does the teams purpose constitute a broader, deeper aspiration than just accomplishing short-term goals?

961. To what degree do the goals specify concrete team work products?

962. To what degree does the teams approach to its work allow for modification and improvement over time?

963. To what degree are the teams goals and objectives clear, simple, and measurable?

964. To what degree are sub-teams possible or necessary?

965. How do you encourage members to learn from each other?

966. To what degree does the teams work approach provide opportunity for members to engage in open interaction?

967. To what degree can the team ensure that all members are individually and jointly accountable for the teams purpose, goals, approach, and work-products?

968. What structural changes have you made or are you preparing to make?

969. Where to from here?

970. Do friends perform better than acquaintances?

971. When does the medium matter?

3.9 Team Member Performance Assessment: Performance testing

972. In what areas would you like to concentrate your knowledge and resources?

973. What are the key duties or tasks of the Ratee?

974. Why do performance reviews?

975. What is the Business Management Oversight Process?

976. What is used as a basis for instructional decisions?

977. How do you determine which data are the most important to use, analyze, or review?

978. How is your organizations Strategic Management System tied to performance measurement?

979. What specific plans do you have for developing effective cross-platform assessments in a blended learning environment?

980. How is performance assessment used in making future award decisions including options and extend/compete decisions?

981. What are the basic principles and objectives of performance measurement and assessment?

982. What happens if a team member receives a Rating of Unsatisfactory?

983. How do you start collaborating?

984. Who should attend?

985. What are top priorities?

986. What stakeholders must be involved in the development and oversight of the performance plan?

987. To what degree can all members engage in open and interactive considerations?

988. What entity leads the process, selects a potential restructuring option and develops the plan?

3.10 Issue Log: Performance testing

989. Can an impact cause deviation beyond team, stage or Performance testing project tolerances?

990. Where do team members get information?

991. What is the status of the issue?

992. How much time does it take to do it?

993. What does the stakeholder need from the team?

994. How do you reply to this question; you am new here and managing this major program. How do you suggest you build your network?

995. What are the stakeholders interrelationships?

996. What effort will a change need?

997. What is the impact on the Business Case?

998. How were past initiatives successful?

999. What help do you and your team need from the stakeholders?

1000. Is the issue log kept in a safe place?

1001. Who were proponents/opponents?

1002. Are there too many who have an interest in some aspect of your work?

1003. Do you feel more overwhelmed by stakeholders?

1004. Who needs to know and how much?

1005. Why not more evaluators?

1006. How often do you engage with stakeholders?

1007. Are you constantly rushing from meeting to meeting?

4.0 Monitoring and Controlling Process Group: Performance testing

1008. How is agile Performance testing project management done?

1009. Did it work?

1010. Were decisions made in a timely manner?

1011. Is the verbiage used appropriate and understandable?

1012. Were escalated issues resolved promptly?

1013. What input will you be required to provide the Performance testing project team?

1014. How can you monitor progress?

1015. How to ensure validity, quality and consistency?

1016. How was the program set-up initiated?

1017. Do clients benefit (change) from the services?

1018. Are there areas that need improvement?

1019. How is Agile Performance testing project Management done?

1020. What departments are involved in its daily operation?

1021. Where is the Risk in the Performance testing project?

1022. Overall, how does the program function to serve the clients?

1023. How do you monitor progress?

1024. How many more potential communications channels were introduced by the discovery of the new stakeholders?

4.1 Project Performance Report: Performance testing

1025. To what degree can team members frequently and easily communicate with one another?

1026. To what degree can team members vigorously define the teams purpose in considerations with others who are not part of the functioning team?

1027. To what degree does the funding match the requirement?

1028. To what degree is the team cognizant of small wins to be celebrated along the way?

1029. To what degree does the formal organization make use of individual resources and meet individual needs?

1030. How will procurement be coordinated with other Performance testing project aspects, such as scheduling and performance reporting?

1031. To what degree can team members meet frequently enough to accomplish the teams ends?

1032. To what degree do members articulate the goals beyond the team membership?

1033. To what degree is there centralized control of information sharing?

1034. To what degree is there a sense that only the team can succeed?

1035. To what degree do team members articulate the teams work approach?

1036. To what degree are the tasks requirements reflected in the flow and storage of information?

1037. To what degree will the approach capitalize on and enhance the skills of all team members in a manner that takes into consideration other demands on members of the team?

1038. To what degree do the relationships of the informal organization motivate taskrelevant behavior and facilitate task completion?

1039. How can Performance testing project sustainability be maintained?

4.2 Variance Analysis: Performance testing

1040. Is the anticipated (firm and potential) business base Performance testing projected in a rational, consistent manner?

1041. Did an existing competitor change strategy?

1042. How are material, labor, and overhead standards set?

1043. At what point should variances be isolated and brought to the attention of the management?

1044. Are estimates of costs at completion generated in a rational, consistent manner?

1045. Why are standard cost systems used?

1046. Are material costs reported within the same period as that in which BCWP is earned for that material?

1047. How are material, labor, and overhead variances calculated and recorded?

1048. Are the overhead pools formally and adequately identified?

1049. Did your organization lose existing customers and/or gain new customers?

1050. Are detailed work packages planned as far in advance as practicable?

1051. What is exceptional?

1052. What is the performance to date and material commitment?

1053. Are data elements reconcilable between internal summary reports and reports forwarded to the stakeholders?

1054. Are all elements of indirect expense identified to overhead cost budgets of Performance testing projections?

1055. Are all authorized tasks assigned to identified organizational elements?

1056. How do you manage changes in the nature of the overhead requirements?

1057. Are all cwbs elements specified for external reporting?

1058. Are indirect costs accumulated for comparison with the corresponding budgets?

4.3 Earned Value Status: Performance testing

1059. Where is evidence-based earned value in your organization reported?

1060. Where are your problem areas?

1061. If earned value management (EVM) is so good in determining the true status of a Performance testing project and Performance testing project its completion, why is it that hardly any one uses it in information systems related Performance testing projects?

1062. How does this compare with other Performance testing projects?

1063. Verification is a process of ensuring that the developed system satisfies the stakeholders agreements and specifications; Are you building the product right? What do you verify?

1064. Validation is a process of ensuring that the developed system will actually achieve the stakeholders desired outcomes; Are you building the right product? What do you validate?

1065. What is the unit of forecast value?

1066. When is it going to finish?

1067. Are you hitting your Performance testing

projects targets?

1068. Earned value can be used in almost any Performance testing project situation and in almost any Performance testing project environment. it may be used on large Performance testing projects, medium sized Performance testing projects, tiny Performance testing projects (in cut-down form), complex and simple Performance testing projects and in any market sector. some people, of course, know all about earned value, they have used it for years - but perhaps not as effectively as they could have?

1069. How much is it going to cost by the finish?

4.4 Risk Audit: Performance testing

1070. Are audit program plans risk-adjusted?

1071. Have staff received necessary training?

1072. Are all managers or operators of the facility or equipment competent or qualified?

1073. Who is responsible for what?

1074. Does the customer understand the process?

1075. Does your organization have or has considered the need for insurance covers: public liability, professional indemnity and directors and officers liability?

1076. What does your data tell you about your risks?

1077. Mitigation -how can you avoid the risk?

1078. Is your organization able to present documentary evidence in support of compliance?

1079. Are your rules, by-laws and practices non-discriminatory?

1080. How do you manage risk?

1081. Does your auditor understand your business?

1082. Are all financial transactions accurately recorded (receipted, banked)?

1083. Are policies communicated to all affected?

1084. Does your organization have a register of insurance policies detailing all current insurance policies?

1085. What is the implication of budget constraint on this process?

1086. Are regular safety inspections made of buildings, grounds and equipment?

1087. Number of users of the product?

4.5 Contractor Status Report: Performance testing

1088. If applicable; describe your standard schedule for new software version releases. Are new software version releases included in the standard maintenance plan?

1089. How long have you been using the services?

1090. Are there contractual transfer concerns?

1091. What was the final actual cost?

1092. What was the overall budget or estimated cost?

1093. Who can list a Performance testing project as organization experience, your organization or a previous employee of your organization?

1094. What is the average response time for answering a support call?

1095. How does the proposed individual meet each requirement?

1096. How is risk transferred?

1097. Describe how often regular updates are made to the proposed solution. Are corresponding regular updates included in the standard maintenance plan?

1098. What are the minimum and optimal bandwidth

requirements for the proposed solution?

1099. What process manages the contracts?

1100. What was the budget or estimated cost for your organizations services?

1101. What was the actual budget or estimated cost for your organizations services?

4.6 Formal Acceptance: Performance testing

1102. What can you do better next time?

1103. Who supplies data?

1104. Does it do what client said it would?

1105. Was the Performance testing project goal achieved?

1106. What function(s) does it fill or meet?

1107. General estimate of the costs and times to complete the Performance testing project?

1108. Did the Performance testing project manager and team act in a professional and ethical manner?

1109. Is formal acceptance of the Performance testing project product documented and distributed?

1110. What are the requirements against which to test, Who will execute?

1111. What lessons were learned about your Performance testing project management methodology?

1112. Do you perform formal acceptance or burn-in tests?

1113. How does your team plan to obtain formal acceptance on your Performance testing project?

1114. Does it do what Performance testing project team said it would?

1115. Was the Performance testing project work done on time, within budget, and according to specification?

1116. Do you buy-in installation services?

1117. Have all comments been addressed?

1118. Was the client satisfied with the Performance testing project results?

1119. Do you buy pre-configured systems or build your own configuration?

1120. What is the Acceptance Management Process?

1121. What features, practices, and processes proved to be strengths or weaknesses?

5.0 Closing Process Group: Performance testing

1122. How well did you do?

1123. Did you do things well?

1124. What is the Performance testing project Management Process?

1125. Who are the Performance testing project stakeholders?

1126. How dependent is the Performance testing project on other Performance testing projects or work efforts?

1127. Did you do what you said you were going to do?

1128. Is there a clear cause and effect between the activity and the lesson learned?

1129. Contingency planning. if a risk event occurs, what will you do?

1130. How well did the chosen processes fit the needs of the Performance testing project?

1131. Is this an updated Performance testing project Proposal Document?

1132. What areas were overlooked on this Performance testing project?

1133. What were the desired outcomes?

1134. What is an Encumbrance?

1135. Will the Performance testing project deliverable(s) replace a current asset or group of assets?

1136. When will the Performance testing project be done?

5.1 Procurement Audit: Performance testing

1137. Does the contract include performance-based clauses?

1138. How do you confirm whether the contracted organization supplied the goods or executed the work as per the quality, quantity and price indicated in the contract agreement/ supply order?

1139. Is the minutes book kept current?

1140. Are purchase orders pre-numbered?

1141. Budget controls: does your organization maintain an up-to-date (approved) budget for all funded activities, and perform a comparison of that budget with actual expenditures for each budget category?

1142. Are regulations and protective measures in place to avoid corruption?

1143. Are the responsibilities of the purchasing department clearly defined?

1144. Can changes be made to automatic disbursement programs without proper approval of management?

1145. Are open purchase orders with a fixed monetary limitation used for local purchases of small dollar value?

1146. Was confidentiality ensured when necessary?

1147. Is the performance of the procurement function/unit regularly evaluated?

1148. Does the strategy include a policy for identifying and training suitable procurement staff?

1149. Is there management monitoring of transactions and balances?

1150. Is the issuance of purchase orders scheduled so that orders are not issued daily?

1151. Were there no material changes in the contract shortly after award?

1152. Was invitation to tender to each specific contract issued after the evaluation of the indicative tenders was completed?

1153. Are individuals with check-signing responsibility prohibited from signing blank checks?

1154. Was suitability of candidates accurately assessed?

1155. Is there a policy covering the relationship of other departments with vendors?

1156. How do you ensure whether the goods were supplied or works executed in time and properly recorded in measurement books and stock/works registers after inspection?

5.2 Contract Close-Out: Performance testing

1157. Have all contracts been closed?

1158. Have all acceptance criteria been met prior to final payment to contractors?

1159. How does it work?

1160. What is capture management?

1161. Has each contract been audited to verify acceptance and delivery?

1162. Why Outsource?

1163. Change in circumstances?

1164. How is the contracting office notified of the automatic contract close-out?

1165. Change in attitude or behavior?

1166. Are the signers the authorized officials?

1167. Was the contract sufficiently clear so as not to result in numerous disputes and misunderstandings?

1168. How/when used ?

1169. Change in knowledge?

1170. Was the contract type appropriate?

1171. Have all contract records been included in the Performance testing project archives?

1172. Parties: who is involved?

1173. Parties: Authorized?

1174. Was the contract complete without requiring numerous changes and revisions?

1175. What happens to the recipient of services?

1176. Have all contracts been completed?

5.3 Project or Phase Close-Out: Performance testing

1177. Who controlled key decisions that were made?

1178. What could have been improved?

1179. What is the information level of detail required for each stakeholder?

1180. Who exerted influence that has positively affected or negatively impacted the Performance testing project?

1181. In preparing the Lessons Learned report, should it reflect a consensus viewpoint, or should the report reflect the different individual viewpoints?

1182. Is the lesson based on actual Performance testing project experience rather than on independent research?

1183. Planned completion date?

1184. What advantages do the an individual interview have over a group meeting, and vice-versa?

1185. What could be done to improve the process?

1186. What were the goals and objectives of the communications strategy for the Performance testing project?

1187. What information is each stakeholder group interested in?

1188. Were risks identified and mitigated?

1189. Complete yes or no?

1190. What was expected from each stakeholder?

1191. Were the outcomes different from the already stated planned?

1192. What was learned?

1193. Was the schedule met?

1194. Who controlled the resources for the Performance testing project?

1195. Which changes might a stakeholder be required to make as a result of the Performance testing project?

5.4 Lessons Learned: Performance testing

1196. How often do communications get lost?

1197. What is the value of the deliverable?

1198. Recommendation: what do you recommend should be done to ensure that others throughout your organization can benefit from what you have learned?

1199. How actively and meaningfully were stakeholders involved in the Performance testing project?

1200. How effectively were issues managed on the Performance testing project?

1201. How clear were you on your role in the Performance testing project?

1202. Were the aims and objectives achieved?

1203. What on the Performance testing project worked well and was effective in the delivery of the product?

1204. What were the main sources of frustration in the Performance testing project?

1205. What are the internal fiscal constraints?

1206. Are corrective actions needed?

1207. Does the lesson describe a function that would be done differently the next time?

1208. What is the supervisor to staff ratio?

1209. How well were your expectations met regarding the extent of your involvement in the Performance testing project (effort, time commitments, etc.)?

1210. What needs to be done over or differently?

1211. Were quality procedures built into the Performance testing project?

1212. How clearly defined were the objectives for this Performance testing project?

1213. How effective was Performance testing project Team member training?

1214. What is your working hypothesis, if you have one?

1215. How effective were Best Practices & Lessons Learned from prior Performance testing projects utilized in this Performance testing project?

Index

287

marked   151
market 22, 166, 202, 250
marketable   202
marketer   7
Marketing   109, 167
markets   22
material   134, 158, 189, 214, 247-248, 260
materials   1, 218
matrices   149
Matrix 3-5, 137, 149, 175, 194, 208
matter 33, 45, 57, 238
maximizing   114
maximum   132
meaningful   51, 119, 202, 237
measurable   29, 36, 158, 198, 238
measure   2, 12, 23-24, 28, 31, 43-45, 48-49, 52, 55, 57-58,
60, 68, 70, 77-78, 80, 83, 87, 89, 95-96, 98, 100, 102, 134, 139, 185,
187
measured   22, 49-52, 55, 59-60, 82, 97, 102, 188, 190
measures   46, 56-58, 60-61, 64, 68, 70, 74-75, 78, 93, 95, 97,
192, 211, 225, 237, 259
measuring   94
mechanical   1
mechanism   224
mechanisms   138-139, 230
medium   238, 250
meeting   28, 97, 187, 192, 196, 212, 223, 233, 235-236, 242,
263
meetings   34, 38, 41, 132, 151, 212, 229, 236
megatrends   112
member   5, 32, 121, 126, 172, 200, 222, 239-240, 266
members   30-31, 34-35, 37, 75, 99, 146, 197, 199-200, 209,
213, 217, 224, 234-238, 240-241, 245-246
membership   245
memorable   237
message   95, 219
messages   201
method   59, 140, 151, 165, 174, 176, 200
methods   36-37, 50, 70, 128, 143, 152, 154, 159, 185, 188,
208, 212
metrics 4, 39, 45, 67, 100, 125, 134, 143, 146, 190-191, 199, 202
milestone   3, 134, 160, 166, 168
milestones   30, 136, 164

CPSIA information can be obtained
at www.ICGtesting.com
Printed in the USA
BVHW071516270619
552031BV00030B/339/P